# THE VOICE
# OF LUKE

## NOT EVEN SANDALS

# BRIAN McLAREN

### WITH DEVOTIONAL NOTES THROUGHOUT

A SCRIPTURE PROJECT TO REDISCOVER THE STORY OF THE BIBLE

THOMAS NELSON
*Since 1798*

NASHVILLE   DALLAS   MEXICO CITY   RIO DE JANEIRO   BEIJING

www.thomasnelson.com

*The Voice of Luke: Not Even Sandals*
©2007 Thomas Nelson, Inc.

the voice.
©2007 Ecclesia Bible Society

Published in Nashville, Tennessee, by Thomas Nelson. Thomas Nelson is a trademark of Thomas Nelson, Inc.


Published in association with Eames Literary Services, Nashville, Tennessee

Typesetting by Rainbow Graphics
Cover Design by Scott Lee Designs (www.scottleedesigns.com)
Cover Photo: Micah Kandros/Scott Lee Designs


*Printed in the United States of America*

2 3 4 5 6 7 8 9—15 14 13 12 11 10 09 08 07

# CONTRIBUTORS

***The Voice of Luke:*** *Not Even Sandals*

SCRIPTURES AND COMMENTARY BY: Brian McLaren

SCHOLARLY REVIEW BY:
David Capes
Darrell L. Bock

EDITORIAL REVIEW BY:
Chris Seay
James F. Couch, Jr.
Maleah Bell
Marilyn Duncan
Amanda Haley
Kelly Hall
Merrie Noland

the voice™

A SCRIPTURE PROJECT TO REDISCOVER THE STORY OF THE BIBLE

# TABLE OF CONTENTS

**Section Two** // Other products from the voice

Any literary project reflects the age in which it is written. **The Voice** is created for and by a church in great transition. Throughout the body of Christ, extensive discussions are ongoing about a variety of issues including style of worship, how we separate culture from our theology, and what is essential truth. In fact, we are struggling with what is truth. At the center of this discussion is the role of Scripture. This discussion is heating up with strong words being exchanged. Instead of furthering the division over culture and theology, it is time to bring the body of Christ together again around the Bible. Thomas Nelson Publishers and Ecclesia Bible Society together are developing Scripture products that foster spiritual growth and theological exploration out of a heart for worship and mission. We have dedicated ourselves to hearing and proclaiming God's voice through this project.

Previously most Bibles and biblical reference works were produced by professional scholars writing in academic settings. **The Voice** uniquely represents collaboration among scholars, pastors, writers, musicians, poets, and other artists. The goal is to create the finest Bible products to help believers experience the joy and wonder of God's revelation. Four key words describe the vision of this project:

- holistic // considers heart, soul, and mind
- beautiful // achieves literary and artistic excellence
- sensitive // respects cultural shifts and the need for accuracy
- balanced // includes theologically diverse writers and scholars

## Uniqueness of *The Voice*

About 40 different human authors are believed to have been inspired by God to write the Scriptures. **The Voice** retains the perspective of the human writers. Most English translations attempt to even out the styles of the different authors in sentence structure and vocabulary. Instead, **The Voice** distinguishes the uniqueness of each author. The heart of the project is retelling the story of the Bible in a form as fluid as modern literary works yet remains true to the original manuscripts. First, accomplished writers create an English rendering; then, respected Bible scholars adjust the rendering to align the manuscript with the original texts. Attention is paid to the use of idioms, artistic elements, confusion of pronouns, repetition of conjunctives, modern sentence structure, and the public reading of the passage. In the process, the writer or scholar may adjust the arrangement of words or expand the phrasing to create an English equivalent.

To help the reader understand how the new rendering of a passage compares to the original manuscripts, several indicators are imbedded within the text. Italic type indicates words not directly tied to a dynamic translation of the original language. Material delineated by a screened box expands on the theme. This portion is not taken directly from the original language. To avoid the endless repetition of simple conjunctives, dialog is formatted as a screenplay. The speaker is indicated, the dialog is indented, and quotation marks are not used. This helps greatly in the public reading of Scripture. Sometimes the original text includes interruptions in the dialog to indicate attitude of the speaker or who is being spoken to. This is shown either as a stage direction immediately following the speaker's name or as part of the narrative section that immediately precedes the speaker's name. The screenplay format clearly shows who is speaking.

Throughout *The Voice,* other language devices improve readability. We follow the standard conventions used in most translations regarding textual evidence. *The Voice* is based on the earliest and best manuscripts from the original languages (Greek, Hebrew, and Aramaic). When significant variations influence a reading, we follow the publishing standard by bracketing the passage and placing a note at the bottom of the page while maintaining the traditional chapter and verse divisions. The footnotes reference quoted material and help the reader understand the translation for a particular word. Words that are borrowed from another language or words that are not common outside of the theological community (such as baptism, repentance, and salvation) are translated into more common terminology. For clarity, some pronouns are replaced with their antecedents. Word order and parts of speech are sometimes altered to help the reader understand the original passage.

— Ecclesia Bible Society

# About *The Voice* Project

As retold, edited, and illustrated by a gifted team
of writers, scholars, poets, and storytellers

## A New Way to Process Ideas

Chris Seay's (president of Ecclesia Bible Society) vision for **The Voice** goes back 15 years to his early attempts to teach the Bible in the narrative as the story of God. As western culture has moved into what is now referred to as postmodernism, Chris observed that the way a new generation processes ideas and information raises obstacles to traditional methods of teaching biblical content. His desire has grown to present the Bible in ways that overcome these obstacles to people coming to faith. Instead of propositional-based thought patterns, people today are more likely to interact with events and individuals through complex observations involving emotions, cognitive processes, tactile experiences, and spiritual awareness. Much as in the parables of Jesus and in the metaphors of the prophets, narrative communication touches the whole person.

Hence, out of that early vision comes the need in a postmodern culture to present Scripture in a narrative form. The result is a retelling of the Scriptures: **The Voice**, not of words, but of meaning and experience.

## The Timeless Narrative

**The Voice** is a fresh expression of the timeless narrative known as the Bible. Stories that were told to emerging generations of God's goodness by their grandparents and tribal leaders were recorded and assembled to form the Christian Scriptures. Too often, the passion, grit, humor, and beauty has been lost in the translation process. **The Voice** seeks to recapture what was lost.

From these early explorations by Chris and others has come **The Voice**: a Scripture project to rediscover the story of the Bible. Thomas Nelson Publishers and Ecclesia Bible Society have joined together to stimulate unique creative experiences and to develop Scripture products and resources to foster spiritual growth and theological exploration out of a heart for the mission of the church and worship of God.

## Traditional Translations

Putting the Bible into the language of modern readers has too often been a painstaking process of correlating the biblical languages to the English vernacular. The Bible is filled with passages intended to inspire, captivate, and depict beauty. The old school of translation most often fails at attempts to communicate beauty, poetry, and story. *The Voice* is a collage of compelling narratives, poetry, song, truth, and wisdom. *The Voice* will call you to enter into the whole story of God with your heart, soul, and mind.

## A New Retelling

One way to describe this approach is to say that it is a "soul translation," not just a "mind translation." But "translation" is not the right word. It is really the retelling of the story. The "retelling" involves translation and paraphrase, but mostly entering into the story of the Scriptures and recreating the event for our culture and time. It doesn't ignore the role of scholars, but it also values the role of writers, poets, songwriters, and artists. Instead, a team of scholars partner with a writer to blend the mood and voice of the original author with an accurate rendering of words of the text in English.

*The Voice* is unique in that it represents collaboration among scholars, writers, musicians, and other artists. Its goal is to create the finest Bible products to help believers experience the joy and wonder of God's revelation. In this time of great transition within the church, we are seeking to give gifted individuals opportunities to craft a variety of products and experiences: a translation of the Scriptures, worship music, worship film festivals, biblical art, worship conferences, gatherings of creative thinkers, a Web site for individuals and churches to share biblical resources, and books derived from exploration during the Bible translation work.

The heart of each product within *The Voice* project is the retelling of the Bible story. To accomplish the objectives of the project and to facilitate the various products envisioned within the project, the Bible text is being translated. We trust that this retelling will be a helpful contribution to a fresh engagement with Scripture. The Bible is the greatest story ever told, but it often doesn't read like it. *The Voice* brings the biblical narratives to life and reads more like a great novel than the traditional versions of the Bible that are seldom opened in contemporary culture.

## Readable and Enjoyable

A careful process is being followed to assure that the spiritual, emotional, and artistic goals of the project are met. First, the retelling of the Bible has been designed to be readable and enjoyable by emphasizing the narrative nature of Scripture. Beyond simply providing a set of accurately translated individual words, phrases, and sentences, our teams were charged to render the biblical texts with sensitivity to the flow of the unfolding story. We asked them to see themselves not only as guardians of the sacred text, but also as storytellers, because we believe that the Bible has always been intended to be heard as the sacred story of the people of God. We assigned each literary unit (for example, the writings of John or Paul) to a team that included a skilled writer and biblical and theological scholars, seeking to achieve a mixture of scholarly expertise and literary skill.

## Personal and Diverse

Second, as a consequence of this team approach, **The Voice** is both personal and diverse. God used about 40 human instruments to communicate His message, and each one has a unique voice or literary style. Standard translations tend to flatten these individual styles so that each book reads more or less like the others—with a kind of impersonal textbook-style prose. Some translations and paraphrases have paid more attention to literary style—but again, the literary style of one writer, no matter how gifted, can unintentionally obscure the diversity of the original voices. To address these problems, we asked our teams to try to feel and convey the diverse literary styles of the original authors.

## Faithful

Third, we have taken care that **The Voice** is faithful and that it avoids prejudice. Anyone who has worked with translation and paraphrase knows that there is no such thing as a completely unbiased or objective translation. So, while we do not pretend to be purely objective, we asked our teams to seek to be as faithful as possible to the biblical message as they understood it together. In addition, as we partnered biblical scholars and theologians with our writers, we intentionally built teams that did not share any single theological tradition. Their diversity has helped each of them not to be trapped within his or her own individual preconceptions, resulting in a faithful and fresh rendering of the Bible.

## Stimulating and Creative

Fourth, we have worked hard to make **The Voice** both stimulating and creative. As we engaged the biblical text, we realized again and again that certain terms have conventional associations for modern readers that would not have been present for the original readers—and that the original readers would have been struck by certain things that remain invisible or opaque to modern readers. Even more, we realized that modern readers from different religious or cultural traditions would hear the same words differently. For example, when Roman Catholic or Eastern Orthodox readers encounter the word "baptism," a very different set of meanings and associations come to mind than those that would arise in the minds of Baptist or Pentecostal readers. And a secular person encountering the text would have still different associations. The situation is made even more complex when we realize that *none* of these associations may resemble the ones that would have come to mind when John invited Jewish peasants and Pharisees into the water of the Jordan River in the months before Jesus began His public ministry. It is far harder than most people realize to help today's readers recapture the original impact of a single word like "baptism." In light of this challenge, we decided, whenever possible, to select words that would stimulate fresh thinking rather than reinforce unexamined assumptions. We want the next generation of Bible readers—whatever their background—to have the best opportunity possible to hear God's message the way the first generation of Bible readers heard it.

## Transformative

Finally, we desire that this translation will be useful and transformative. It is all too common in many of our Protestant churches to have only a few verses of biblical text read in a service, and then that selection too often becomes a jumping-off point for a sermon that is at best peripherally related to, much less rooted in, the Bible itself. The goal of **The Voice** is to promote the public reading of longer sections of Scripture—followed by thoughtful engagement with the biblical narrative in its richness and fullness and dramatic flow. We believe the Bible itself, in all its diversity and energy and dynamism, is the message; it is not merely the jumping-off point.

The various creations of the project bring creative application of commentary and interpretive tools. These are clearly indicated and separated from the Bible text that is drawn directly from traditional sources. Along with the creative resources and fresh expressions of God's Word, the reader has the benefit of centuries of biblical research applied dynamically to our rapidly changing culture.

The products underway in ***The Voice*** include dynamic and interactive presentations of the critical passages in the life of Jesus and the early church, recorded musical presentation of Scripture originally used in worship or uniquely structured for worship, artwork commissioned from young artists, dramatized audio presentations from the Gospels and the Old Testament historical books, film commentary on our society using the words of Scripture, and exploration of the voice of each human author of the Bible.

The first product for ***The Voice***, entitled *The Last Eyewitness: The Final Week*, released Spring 2006, follows Jesus through His final week of life on earth through the firsthand account of John the apostle. This book combines the drama of the text with the artwork of Rob Pepper into a captivating retelling of Jesus' final days. The second product, *The Dust Off Their Feet: Lessons from the First Church*, was released September 2006 and includes the entire Book of Acts retold by Brian McLaren with commentary and articles written by nine scholars and pastors. *The Voice of Matthew* was released January 2007 with the Gospel of Matthew retold by Lauren Winner including Lauren's devotional commentary, along with cultural and historical notes. For excerpts from these books, see the back of this book.

*The Voice from on High* will be published in the fall of 2007 with over 700 verses from 19 Old Testament and New Testament books. The story of the Liberating King is shown to run through the Bible from Genesis to Revelation. Over a dozen writers are contributing to the retelling of the Scriptures with special notes by Jonathan Hal Reynolds. *The Voice Revealed* is the full Gospel of John retold by Chris Seay in a compact edition to introduce others to the faith. *The Voice of Hebrews: The Mystery of Melchizedek* includes a retelling of the Book of Hebrews by Greg Garrett with extensive notes and articles by David Capes. *The Voice of Mark* retold by Greg Garrett with commentary by Matthew Paul Turner will complete the products for the winter.

## The Team

The team writing ***The Voice*** brings unprecedented gifts to this unique project. An award-winning fiction writer, an acclaimed poet, a pastor renowned for using art and narrative in his preaching and teaching, Greek and Hebrew authorities, and biblical scholars are all coming together to capture the beauty and diversity of God's Word.

## Writers

The contributors to *The Voice of Luke: Not Even Sandals* are:

**Brian McLaren**—Internationally known speaker and author of more than a dozen books, including *A New Kind of Christian, A Generous Orthodoxy, The Secret Message of Jesus,* and *The Dust Off Their Feet: Lessons from the First Church.*

along with two critical reviewers:

**David Capes, PhD**—Chair of the Department of Christianity and Philosophy at Houston Baptist University. He has written several books, including *The Footsteps of Jesus in the Holy Land.*

and

**Darrell L. Bock, PhD**—Research Professor of New Testament Studies at Dallas Theological Seminary, Elder Emeritus at Trinity Fellowship Church, Contributing Editor at *Christianity Today,* and author of commentaries on Mark, Luke, and Acts, as well as of a book on Jesus and Scripture.

Writers for ***The Voice*** include:

**Eric Bryant**—pastor/author
**David Capes**—professor/author
**Tara Leigh Cobble**—singer/songwriter
**Don Chaffer**—singer/songwriter/poet
**Lori Chaffer**—singer/songwriter/poet
**Robert Creech**—pastor/author
**Greg Garrett**— professor/author
**Christena Graves**—singer
**Sara Groves**—singer/songwriter
**Amanda Haley**—archaeology scholar/editor

**Charlie Hall**—singer/songwriter
**Kelly Hall**—editor/poet
**Justin Hyde**—pastor/author
**Andrew Jones**— pastor/consultant
**E. Chad Karger**—counselor/author/pastor
**Tim Keel**—pastor
**Greg LaFollette**—musician/songwriter
**Evan Lauer**—pastor/author
**Phuc Luu**—chaplain/adjunct instructor
**Christian McCabe**—pastor/artist
**Donald Miller**—author
**Sean Palmer**—pastor
**Jonathan Hal Reynolds**—poet
**Chris Seay**—pastor/author
**Robbie Seay**—singer/songwriter
**Kerry Shook**—pastor
**Chuck Smith, Jr.**—pastor/author
**Allison Smythe**—poet
**Leonard Sweet**—author
**Kristin Swenson**—professor/author
**Phyllis Tickle**—author
**Matthew Paul Turner**—author/speaker
**Lauren Winner**—lecturer/author
**Seth Woods**—singer/songwriter
**Dieter Zander**—pastor/author

## Scholars

Other biblical and theological scholars for ***The Voice*** include:

**Joseph Blair, ThD**—professor
**Alan Culpepper, PhD**—dean/professor
**Peter H. Davids, PhD**—pastor/professor
**J. R. Dodson**—adjunct professor
**Brett Dutton, PhD**—pastor/adjunct professor
**Dave Garber, PhD**—professor
**Charlie Harvey, PhD**—assistant professor

**Peter Rhea Jones, Sr., PhD**—pastor/professor
**Sheri Klouda, PhD**—professor
**Creig Marlowe, PhD**—dean/professor
**Troy Miller, PhD**—professor
**Frank Patrick**—assistant professor
**Chuck Pitts, PhD**—professor
**Felisi Sorgwe, PhD**—pastor/professor
**Jack Wisdom, JD**—lawyer
**Nancy de Claissé Walford, PhD**—professor
**Kenneth Waters, Sr., PhD**—professor

# A WORD ABOUT THIS BOOK...

When it came time for Jesus to send out His disciples in pairs to the surrounding towns, He said,

> There's a great harvest waiting in the fields, but there aren't many good workers to harvest it. Pray that the Harvest Master will send out good workers to the fields.
> It's time for you 70 to go. I'm sending you out *armed with vulnerability*, like lambs walking into a pack of wolves. Don't bring a wallet. Don't carry a backpack. I don't even want you to wear sandals. Walk along *barefoot, quietly,* without stopping for small talk. When you enter a house seeking lodging, say, "Peace on this house!" If a child of peace—one who welcomes God's message of peace—is there, your peace will rest on him. If not, don't worry; nothing is wasted. Stay where you're welcomed. *Become part of the family,* eating and drinking whatever they give you.                                    Luke 10:2–7

Jesus was calling His disciples to a whole new level of commitment. They were to depend on the Lord and His mission for everything. They were to "walk along barefoot, quietly." Later, at the end of His ministry, Jesus reminds the disciples and Peter in particular about His commission for them, "Remember when I sent you out with no money, no pack, not even sandals? Did you lack anything?" (22:35). As we considered the significance of Jesus' radical invitation, we chose *Not Even Sandals* as the subtitle for this work. It reflects the courageous dedication of the first disciples as uniquely revealed in Luke's Gospel, and it speaks to our need for commitment to the mission of Jesus.

With each book or group of books of the Bible in **The Voice**, we seek to find the proper match of voice, or style, of the original biblical writer and of the writer chosen to retell the story. Each of the four Gospels has its own style and unique purpose: Matthew is a very Jewish Gospel; it seeks to prove through Old Testament quotations and allusions that Jesus is the Liberating King from birth. Matthew presents Jesus as a new Moses who ascends the mountain and writes a new law on the hearts of His disciples. So we chose Lauren Winner, who was raised an orthodox Jew, to retell the story found in Matthew. You can read her thrilling account in *The Voice of Matthew*. Mark is a fast-paced story told in a simple, straightforward writing style. Mark shows that Jesus' entire life and ministry was the mustard seed stage of the gospel as it invites us to grow with him in faithful discipleship. In turn, we chose a novelist, Greg Garrett, to retell Mark. Greg goes to great lengths to reflect Mark's brief yet powerful style. John, too, is a simple but elegant story. The symbolism and imagery used in this Gospel underscore in a beautiful and timeless fashion that Jesus is the true Liberating King, the heavenly Son of God who has come to reveal the Father. Chris Seay took on the task of retelling John, since he has written several books that speak evangelistically to our culture. But Luke is the master storyteller. He presents a seamless history from the conception of John the Immerser through the imprisonment of Paul. You see Luke didn't write just one book. The sometime missionary-associate of Paul also wrote the longest book in the New Testament, the Acts of the Apostles. We presented that story in *The Dust Off Their Feet*. Luke's style is refined and sophisticated—more than most other New Testament writers—and his purpose is clear: to present Jesus as the perfect man, a new Adam, the model of a new humanity.

Choosing Brian McLaren to retell his story was not a difficult decision. His writing style is clearly similar to Luke's. The attention given to detail, the awareness of the contemporary culture, and the role of the Gentile church are paralleled in Brian's work. Brian McLaren best represents the refined physician who documented the history of Jesus and those who pioneered the church.

Our goal is for you to experience the richness of the story told by Luke and for you to see yourself as a revolutionary like the disciples, who were willing to depend completely upon their Lord and serve Him. So you too may follow Him with no money, no pack, not even sandals.

— Ecclesia Bible Society

Section One // **The Book of Luke**

# FOR THOSE WHO LOVE GOD

*W*hat are your assumptions as you begin this amazing document? What do you assume about Luke as an author—his motives, his agenda, his assumptions? Any constructive experience of reading involves an amazing interaction so complex that it's a wonder it ever works at all. First, there are readers across time and space, each reading with certain questions, certain assumptions, and a certain worldview. Then there's an author, located in another specific time and place, embedded in his own context and worldview. The author and the readers also come from communities or traditions—groups of people who share their basic worldview and who teach them to think, write, read, and respond in certain ways.

In all my years of reading (and writing), I've concluded that we as readers have the obligation to try to enter the writer's world, to understand him on his own terms and in his own context, rather than requiring him to enter ours (something he can't do!). That means that we need to try to imagine Luke's world. Fortunately, we have Luke's sequel to this Gospel to help us understand more about him. (It's called the Acts of the Apostles, and the two documents shed light on each other.) Tradition tells us that Luke is a physician, active in the early church in the years around A.D. 60. He travels widely with the emissary Paul; so he is a sort of cosmopolitan person, multicultural in his sensitivities, understanding both Jewish culture and the broader Greco-Roman culture of the Roman Empire. As a physician, he is more educated than the average person of his day, but I think you'll be impressed with his ability to relate to common people—and especially his skill as a storyteller. Remember that Luke isn't presenting us with a theological treatise (as good and important as theological treatises may be); he's telling us the story of Jesus, gathered from many eyewitnesses. Based on the intended audience of his book (Theophilus—literally, God-lover), we can assume he wants to help people who love God to love Him even more by knowing what He has done through Jesus.

¹⁻³For those who love God, several other people have already written accounts of what God has been bringing to completion among us, using the reports of the original eyewitnesses, those who were there from the start to witness the fulfillment of prophecy. Like those other servants who have recorded the messages, I present to you my carefully researched, orderly account of these new teachings. ⁴I want you to know that you can fully rely on the things you have been taught *about Jesus, God's Anointed One.*

⁵*To understand the life of Jesus, I must first give you some background history, events that occurred when* Herod ruled Judea *for the Roman Empire*. Zacharias was serving as a priest *in the temple in Jerusalem* those days as his fathers had before him. He was a member of the priestly division of Abijah *(a grandson of Aaron who innovated temple practices)*, and his wife, Elizabeth, was of the priestly lineage of Aaron, *Moses' brother.* ⁶They were good and just people in God's sight, walking with integrity in the Lord's ways and laws. ⁷Yet they had this sadness. Due to Elizabeth's infertility, they were childless,

and at this time, they were both quite old—*well past normal childbearing years.*

*I*n the time of Jesus, Jewish life was centered in the temple in Jerusalem. The temple was staffed by religious professionals, what we might refer to as "clergy" today, called priests. They were responsible for the temple's activities—which included receiving religious pilgrims and their sacrifices (cattle, sheep, goats, and doves). Animal sacrifices sound strange to us—we often associate them with some kind of extremist cult. But in the ancient world, they were quite common. It may help, in trying to understand animal sacrifices, to remember that the slaughter of animals was a daily experience in the ancient world; it was part of any meal that included meat. So perhaps we should think of the sacrifice of animals as, first and foremost, a special meal. This meal brings together the Jewish family from near and far, seeking to affirm their connection to the one true and living God. Their gift of animals was their contribution to the meal. (The priests, by the way, were authorized to use the meat for the sustenance of their families.)

The presentation of the blood and meat of these sacrifices was accompanied by a number of prescribed rituals, performed by priests wearing prescribed ornamental clothing, according to a prescribed schedule. As the story continues, we see these solemn rituals interrupted in a most unprecedented way.

⁸One day, Zacharias was chosen to perform his priestly duties in God's presence, according to the temple's normal schedule and

routine. [9]He had been selected from all the priests by the customary procedure of casting lots *for a once-in-a-lifetime opportunity* to enter the sacred precincts of the temple. There he burned sweet incense, [10]while outside a large crowd of people prayed. [11]*Suddenly, Zacharias realized he was not alone:* a messenger of the Lord was there with him. The messenger stood just to the right of the altar of incense. [12]Zacharias was shocked and afraid, [13]but the messenger reassured him.

**Messenger** | Zacharias, calm down! Don't be afraid!

*A*gain and again, when people encounter God (or when they receive a message from God, often through a vision of a heavenly messenger), their first response is terror; and so they need to be calmed down before they can receive the message. We might think Zacharias shouldn't be surprised to hear from God; after all, he's a priest working in the temple. But priests didn't normally hear from God. Those who heard from God were called prophets, not priests.

Priests worked "the family business," so to speak. One became a priest by being born in a priestly family line. Prophets, on the other hand, arose unpredictably. Prophets had no special credentials except the message they carried. So Zacharias had no reason to believe his duties would be interrupted in this way.

Often in the biblical story, when people receive a message from God, after getting over the initial shock, they start asking questions. They push back; they doubt. However, when the word of the Lord comes to people, it doesn't turn them into unthinking zombies or robots; it doesn't override their individuality or capacity to think. Perhaps many of us in some way hear the voice of the Lord, but we don't realize it because we're expecting lightning flashes and a voice with a lot of reverb, a voice so overpowering that we are incapable of questioning and doubting it.

**Messenger** | Zacharias, your prayers have been heard. Your wife is going to have a son, and you will name him John. [14]He will bring you great joy and happiness—and many will share your joy at John's birth.

[15]This son of yours will be a great man in God's sight. He will not drink alcohol in any form; *instead of alcoholic spirits*, he will be filled with the Holy Spirit from the time he is in his mother's womb. [16]*Here is his mission: he will stop many of the children of Israel in their misguided paths, and* he'll turn them around to follow the path to the Lord their God instead.

[17]Do you remember the prophecy about someone to come in the spirit and power of the prophet Elijah; someone who will turn the hearts of the parents back to their children;* someone who will turn the hearts of the disobedient to the mind-set of the just and good? Your son is the one who will fulfill this prophecy: he will be the Lord's forerunner, the one who will prepare the people and make them ready for God.

---

1:17 Malachi 4:5-6

*We* mentioned that Luke was a master storyteller, so we've decided to contextualize his method of storytelling to our own culture in some creative ways. First, we'll highlight dialogue (as you'll see we do in this episode), rendering Luke's account in the form of a screenplay. Second, from time to time, we'll have Luke say, "Picture this," or "Imagine this." Then we'll use present tense to help you enter the story imaginatively, as if you were there yourself.

**Zacharias** | [18]How can I be sure of what you're telling me? I am an old man, and my wife is far past the normal age for women to bear children. *This is hard to believe!*

**Messenger** | [19]I am Gabriel, the messenger who inhabits God's
*(sternly)* | presence. I was sent here to talk with you and bring you this good news. [20]Because you didn't believe my message, you will not be able to talk—not another word—until you experience the fulfillment of my words.

[21]Meanwhile, the crowd at the temple wondered why Zacharias hadn't come out of the sanctuary yet. It wasn't normal for the priest to be delayed so long. [22]When at last he came out, *it was clear from his face something had happened in there.* He was making signs with his hands to give the blessing, but he couldn't speak. They realized he had seen some sort of vision. [23]When his time on duty at the temple came to an end, he went back home to his wife. [24]Shortly after his return, Elizabeth became pregnant. She avoided public contact for the next five months.

**Elizabeth** | ²⁵I have lived with the disgrace of being barren for all these years. Now God has looked on me with favor. When I go out in public *with my baby*, I will not be disgraced any longer.

²⁶Six months later in Nazareth, a city in *the rural province of* Galilee, the heavenly messenger Gabriel made another appearance. This time, the messenger was sent by God ²⁷to meet with a virgin named Mary, who was engaged to a man named Joseph, a descendant of King David himself. ²⁸The messenger entered her home.

**Messenger** | Greetings! You are favored, and the Lord is with you! [Among all women on the earth you have been blessed.]*

²⁹The heavenly messenger's words baffled Mary, and she wondered what type of greeting this was.

**Messenger** | ³⁰Mary, don't be afraid. You have found favor with God. ³¹Listen, you are going to become pregnant. You will have a Son, and you must name Him "Liberation," *or* Jesus.* ³²Jesus will become the greatest among men. He will be known as the Son of the Highest God. God will give Him the throne of His ancestor David, ³³and He will reign over the covenant family of Jacob forever.

---

1:28 The earliest manuscripts omit this portion.
1:31 Through the naming of Jesus, God is speaking prophetically about the role Jesus will play in our salvation.

**Mary** | ³⁴But I have never been with a man. How can this be possible?

**Messenger** | ³⁵The Holy Spirit will come upon you. The Most High will overshadow you. That's why this holy child will be known, *as not just your son, but also* as the Son of God. ³⁶*It sounds impossible,* but listen—you know your relative Elizabeth has been unable to bear children and is now far too old to be a mother. Yet she has become pregnant, *as God willed it.* Yes, in three months, she will have a son. ³⁷So the impossible is possible with God.

**Mary**
*(deciding in her heart)* | ³⁸Here I am, the Lord's humble servant. As you have said, let it be done to me.

*L*uke is very interested in the ways that disadvantaged people of his day—the poor, the sick, and women—respond to God. Already, we see a fascinating interplay between Zacharias's response to God and Mary's. If you compare them, you'll see how their responses are similar in some ways but very different in others.

And the heavenly messenger was gone. ³⁹Mary immediately got up and hurried to the hill country, in the province of Judah, ⁴⁰⁻⁴¹where her cousins Zacharias and Elizabeth lived. When Mary entered their home and greeted Elizabeth, who felt her baby leap in her womb, Elizabeth was filled with the Holy Spirit.

**Elizabeth**   | [42]You are blessed, Mary, blessed among all women,
*(shouting)*    | and the child you bear is blessed! [43]And blessed I am
as well, that the mother of my Lord has come to
me! [44]As soon as I heard your voice greet me, my
baby leaped for joy within me. [45]How fortunate you
are, Mary, for you believed that what the Lord told
you would be fulfilled.

*M*ary is deeply moved by these amazing encounters—first
with the messenger and then with her cousin, Elizabeth. Mary's response can't be contained in normal prose; her noble soul overflows in poetry. And this poetry isn't simply religious; it has powerful social and political overtones. It speaks of a great reversal—what we might call a social, economic, and political revolution. To people in Mary's day, there would be little question as to what she was talking about. The Jewish people were oppressed by the Roman Empire, and to speak of a Liberator who would demote the powerful and rich and elevate the poor and humble would mean one thing: God was moving toward setting them free! Soon we'll hear Zacharias overflowing in poetry of his own.

**Mary**  | [46]My soul lifts up the Lord!
[47]My spirit celebrates God, my Liberator!
[48]For though I'm God's humble servant,
God has noticed me.
Now and forever,
I will be considered blessed by all generations.

49For the Mighty One has done great things for me;
　　holy is God's name!
50From generation to generation,
　　God's lovingkindness endures
　　for those who revere Him.


51God's arm has accomplished mighty deeds.
　　The proud in mind and heart,
　　God has sent away in disarray.
52The rulers from their high positions of power,
　　God has brought down low.
　And those who were humble and lowly,
　　God has elevated with dignity.
53The hungry—God has filled with fine food.
　The rich—God has dismissed with nothing in
　　their hands.
54To Israel, God's servant,
　　God has given help,
55As promised to our ancestors,
　　remembering Abraham and his descendants in
　　mercy forever.


56Mary stayed with Elizabeth *in Judea* for the next three months and then returned to her home *in Galilee*.

57Three months later, Elizabeth gave birth to a son. 58News about the Lord's special kindness to her had spread through her extended family and the community. Everyone shared her joy, *for after all these years of infertility, she had a son!* 59*As was customary,* eight days after the baby's birth the time came for his circumcision *and naming*. Everyone assumed he would be named Zacharias, like his father.

**Elizabeth**  |  ⁶⁰No. We will name him John.
*(disagreeing)*  |


**Her Relatives**  |  ⁶¹That name is found nowhere in your family.
*(protesting)*  |


⁶²They turned to Zacharias and asked him what he wanted the baby's name to be.

⁶³He motioned for a tablet, and he wrote, "His name is John." Everyone was shocked *by this breach of family custom. ⁶⁴They were even more surprised when,* at that moment, Zacharias was able to talk again, and he shouted out praises to God. ⁶⁵A sense of reverence spread through the whole community. In fact, this story was spread throughout the hilly countryside of Judea. ⁶⁶People were certain that God's hand was on this child, and they wondered what sort of person John would turn out to be when he became a man.

⁶⁷When Zacharias's voice was restored to him, he spoke from the fullness of the Spirit a prophetic utterance.


**Zacharias**  |  ⁶⁸May the Lord God of Israel be blessed indeed!
For God's intervention has begun,
and He has moved to rescue us,
the people of God.
⁶⁹And the Lord has raised up a powerful sign of
liberation for us
from among the descendants of God's servant,
*King* David.
⁷⁰As was prophesied through the mouths of His
holy prophets in ancient times:

⁷¹*God will* liberate us "from our enemies"*
    and "from the hand of our oppressors!"*

⁷²⁻⁷⁴God will show mercy promised to our ancestors,
    upholding the abiding covenant He made with
        them,
    Remembering the original vow He swore to
        Abraham,
        from whom we are all descended.
    God will grant us liberation from the grasp of our
        enemies,
        so that we may serve Him without fear all our
            days
⁷⁵In holiness and justice, in the presence of the
    Lord.

⁷⁶And you, my son, will be called the prophet of the
    Most High.
    For you will be the one to prepare the way for
        the Lord,*
⁷⁷So that the Lord's people will receive knowledge
    of their liberation
    through the forgiveness of their sins.

⁷⁸All this will flow from the kind and compassionate
    mercy of our God.

---

1:71 Psalm 106:10
1:71 Psalm 106:10
1:76 Isaiah 40:3

> *A new day is dawning:*
>     the Sunrise from the heavens will break
>         through in our darkness,
> <sup>79</sup>And those who huddle in night,
>     those who sit in the shadow of death,
> *Will be able to rise* and walk in the light,*
>     guided in the pathway of peace.

<sup>80</sup>And John grew up and became strong in spirit. He lived in the wilderness, *outside the cities,* until the day came for him to step into the public eye in Israel.

---

# *Luke 2*

## THE HUMBLE AND THE POOR
## GREET THEIR KING

[1]Around the time *of Elizabeth's amazing pregnancy and John's birth, the emperor in Rome,* Caesar Augustus, required everyone in the Roman Empire to participate in a massive census—[2]the first census since Quirinius had become governor of Syria. [3]Each person had to go to his or her ancestral city to be counted.

*R*emember—for the original hearers of this story, this political background wasn't incidental: it was crucial to the story. Conquering nations in the ancient world worked in various ways. Some brutally destroyed and plundered the nations they conquered. Some took conquered people as slaves or servants. Other empires allowed the people to remain in their land and work as before, but with one major change: the conquered people would have to pay taxes to their rulers. The purpose of a census like the one Luke describes was to be sure that everyone was appropriately taxed and knew ultimately who was in charge.

[4-5]Mary's fiancé Joseph, from Nazareth in Galilee, had to participate in the census in the same way *everyone else did.* Because he was a descendant of *King* David, his ancestral city was Bethlehem, David's birthplace. Mary, who was now late in her pregnancy *which the messenger Gabriel had predicted,* [6]accompanied Joseph. While in Bethlehem,

she went into labor [7]and gave birth to her firstborn son. She
wrapped the baby in a blanket and laid Him in a feeding trough because the inn had no room for them.

[8]Nearby, in the fields outside of Bethlehem, a group of shepherds
were guarding their flocks *from predators* in the darkness of night.
[9]Suddenly, a messenger of the Lord stood in front of them, and the
darkness was replaced by a glorious light—the shining light of
God's glory. They were terrified!

Messenger | [10]Don't be afraid! Listen! I bring good news, news of
great joy, news that will affect all people everywhere. [11]Today, in the city of David, a Liberator has
been born for you! He is the promised Liberating
King, the Supreme Authority! [12]You will know you
have found Him when you see a baby, wrapped in a
blanket, lying in a feeding trough.

[13]At that moment, the first heavenly messenger was joined by
thousands of other messengers—a vast heavenly choir. They praised
God.

Heavenly | [14]To the highest heights of the universe, glory to
Choir |      God!
And on earth, peace among all people who
bring pleasure to God!

[15]As soon as the heavenly messengers disappeared into heaven,
the shepherds were buzzing with conversation.

**Shepherds** | Let's rush down to Bethlehem right now! Let's see
what's happening! Let's experience what the Lord
has told us about!

¹⁶So they ran into town, and *eventually* they found Mary and
Joseph and the baby lying in the feeding trough. After they saw the
baby, ¹⁷they spread the story of *what they had experienced and* what had
been said to them about this child. ¹⁸Everyone who heard their story
couldn't stop thinking about its meaning. ¹⁹Mary too pondered all of
these events, treasuring each memory in her heart.

²⁰The shepherds returned *to their flocks*, praising God for all
they had seen and heard, and they glorified God for the way the
experience had unfolded just as the heavenly messenger had
predicted.

*R*emember what we said about Luke's fascination with
disadvantaged people? Here we have it again. Jesus' first visitors
were not ambassadors, dignitaries, or wealthy landowners. The
first to pay Him homage were simple shepherds, minimum-wage
workers in the ancient agrarian economy. They had little to no
status in the world. They were the humble and the poor whom
God was now raising up to receive heavenly messages and an
audience with the great King. Watch for this theme as the story
continues.

²¹Eight days after His birth, the baby was circumcised *in keeping
with Jewish religious requirements,* and He was named Jesus, the name

the messenger had given Him before His conception in Mary's womb. [22]After Mary had observed the ceremonial days of *postpartum* purification required by Mosaic law, she and Joseph brought Jesus to the temple in Jerusalem to present Him to the Lord. [23]They were fulfilling the Lord's requirement that "every firstborn *Israelite* male will be dedicated to the Eternal One as holy."* [24]They also offered the sacrifice required by the law of the Lord, "two turtledoves or two young pigeons."*

[25]*While fulfilling these sacred obligations at the temple,* they encountered a man in Jerusalem named Simeon. He was a just and pious man, anticipating the liberation of Israel from her troubles. He was a man in touch with the Holy Spirit. [26]The Holy Spirit had revealed to Simeon that he would not die before he had seen the Lord's Liberating King. [27]The Spirit had led him to the temple that day, and there he saw the child Jesus in the arms of His parents, who were fulfilling their sacred obligations. [28]Simeon took Jesus into his arms and blessed God.

> **Simeon** | [29]Now, Lord *and King,* You can let me,
> Your humble servant, die in peace.
> [30]You promised me that I would see with my own eyes
> what I'm seeing now: Your liberation,
> [31]Raised up in the presence of all peoples.
> [32]He is the light who reveals Your message to the
> other nations,
> and He is the shining glory of Your *covenant*
> people, Israel.

---

**2:23** Exodus 13:2,12,15
**2:24** Leviticus 12:8

[33]His father and mother were stunned to hear Simeon say these things. [34]Simeon went on to bless them both, and to Mary in particular he gave predictions.

> Simeon | Listen, this child will make many in Israel rise and fall. He will be a significant person whom many will oppose. [35]*In the end,* He will lay bare the secret thoughts of many hearts. And a sword will pierce even your own soul, Mary.

[36]At that very moment, an elderly woman named Anna stepped forward. Anna was a prophetess, the daughter of Phanuel, of the tribe of Asher. She had been married for seven years *before her husband died,* [37]and she was a widow to her current age of 84 years. She was *deeply devoted to the Lord,* constantly in the temple, fasting and praying. [38]When she approached *Mary, Joseph, and Jesus,* she began speaking out thanks to God, and she continued spreading the word about Jesus to all those who shared her hope for the liberation of Jerusalem.

[39]After fulfilling their sacred duties according to the law of the Lord, Mary and Joseph returned *with Jesus* to their own city of Nazareth in the province of Galilee. [40]There Jesus grew up, maturing in physical strength and increasing in wisdom, and the grace of God rested on Him.

[41]Every year *during Jesus' childhood*, His parents traveled to Jerusalem for the Passover celebration. [42]When Jesus was 12, He made the journey with them. [43]They spent several days there, participating in the whole celebration. When His parents left for home, Jesus stayed in Jerusalem, but Joseph and Mary were not aware. [44]They

assumed Jesus was elsewhere in the caravan *that was traveling together*. After they had already traveled a full day's journey *toward home*, they began searching for Him among their friends and relatives. ⁴⁵When no one had seen the boy, Mary and Joseph rushed back to Jerusalem and searched for Him.

⁴⁶After three days of separation, they finally found Him—sitting among a group of religious teachers in the temple, *deep in the give-and-take of serious conversation*—asking them questions, listening to their answers, *and answering the questions they asked Him*. ⁴⁷Everyone was surprised and impressed that a 12-year-old boy could have such deep understanding and could answer questions *with such wisdom*.

⁴⁸His parents, of course, had a different reaction.

> **Mary** | Son, why have You treated us this way? Listen, Your father and I have been sick with worry *for the last three days, wondering where You were*, looking everywhere for You.

> **Jesus** | ⁴⁹Why did you need to look for Me? Didn't you know that I must be working for My Father?

*W*e are told so little about Jesus' life between His birth and the age of 30. But this one episode tells us so much. First, it tells us that Jesus' family life was a lot like our own—full of mishaps and misunderstandings. Second, it tells us that as Jesus entered young adulthood, He began manifesting an extraordinary sense of identity. (Remember, a 12-year-old wasn't "just a kid" in those days—he was becoming a man.) He wasn't just "Mary's boy" or "Joseph's stepson."

> He had a direct relationship with God as His Father, and He knew
> that His life would follow a path of working for God.

[50]Neither Mary nor Joseph really understood what He meant by this. [51]Jesus went back to Nazareth with them and was obedient to them. His mother continued to store these memories like treasures in her heart. [52]And Jesus kept on growing—in wisdom, in physical stature, in favor with God, and in favor with others.

# *Luke 3*

## JOHN SPEAKS OF COMING WRATH

*M*ore than any other Gospel writer, Luke wants to situate the story of the Liberating King in what we might call "secular history." In particular, he gives us details of the emperor, governor, and other client rulers. With a toxic mixture of cruelty and might, these authorities lorded over the common people. Yet these high and mighty are—if you remember Mary's poem—destined to be brought down in the presence of a new kind of king and a new kind of kingdom. Jesus will exercise His authority in a radically different way—not through domination and violence, but through love, healing, compassion, and service.

¹Our story continues 15 years after Tiberius Caesar had begun his reign over the empire. Pilate was governor of Judea, Herod ruled Galilee, his brother Philip ruled Ituraea and Trachonitis, and Lysanias ruled Abilene. ²*In Jerusalem,* Annas and Caiaphas were high priests in the temple. And in those days, out in the wilderness, John (son of Zacharias) received a message from God.

³John brought this divine message to all those who came to the Jordan River. He preached that people should be ritually washed* as an expression of changed lives for the forgiveness of sins. ⁴As Isaiah the prophet had said,

---

**3:3** Literally, immersion, an act of repentance

A solitary voice is calling:
"Go into the wilderness,
     prepare the road for the Eternal One's journey,
In the desert, repair and straighten
     every mile of our True God's highway.
⁵Every low place will be lifted
     and every high mountain,
     every hill will be humbled;
The crooked road will be straightened out
     and rough places ironed out smooth;
⁶Then the radiant glory of the Eternal One will be revealed.
     All flesh together will take it in."*

⁷In fulfillment of those words, crowds streamed out *from the villages and towns* to be ritually washed* by John *at the Jordan.*

*Y*ou'll remember that Zacharias was a priest who served in Jerusalem at the temple. Among their other duties, priests would perform ritual cleansings necessary for Jewish worshipers who had become ceremonially unclean—perhaps through contact with outsiders (non-Jewish people), perhaps through contact with blood or a dead body, perhaps through a physical illness. Near the temple, archaeologists have found many of the baths or pools that were used for these ceremonial cleansings. But notice that when John appears on the scene, he hasn't followed in his father's footsteps. He's not fulfilling the role of the priest, but rather of the prophet. He works

---

**3:4-6** Isaiah 40:3-5
**3:7** Literally, immersion, an act of repentance

far outside of Jerusalem, and he baptizes people in the Jordan River, not near the temple. It's as if John is performing a symbolic drama: If you want to be in tune with God, the temple and its normal routines can't help you anymore. Instead of being cleansed there, you should come out to this radical preacher and let him cleanse you in the river. And his message, as you're about to see, isn't a polite, tame message. It's fiery and intense! God isn't interested in just routine religion. He wants changed lives!

**John the Preacher** | You bunch of venomous snakes! Who told you that you could escape God's coming wrath? [8]Don't just talk of turning to God; you'd better bear the authentic fruit of a changed life. Don't take pride in your religious heritage, saying, "We have Abraham for our father!" Listen—God could turn these rocks into children of Abraham!

[9]*Face the facts, people! God is fed up with religious talk. God wants you to bear fruit!* If you don't produce good fruit, then you'll be chopped down like a fruitless tree and made into firewood. God's axe is taking aim and ready to swing!

**People** | [10]What shall we do *to perform works from changed lives?*

**John the Preacher** | [11]The person who has two shirts must share with the person who has none. And the person with food must share with the one in need.

¹²Some tax collectors were among those in the crowd seeking ritual washing.*

**Tax Collectors** | Teacher, what kind of fruit is God looking for from us?

**John the Preacher** | ¹³Stop overcharging people. Only collect what you must turn over to the Romans.

**Soldiers** | ¹⁴What about us? What should we do *to show true change*?

**John the Preacher** | Don't extort money from people by throwing around your power or making false accusations, and be content with your pay.

¹⁵John's bold message seized public attention, and many began wondering if John might himself be the Liberating King *promised by God.*

**John the Preacher** | ¹⁶*I am not the One.* I ritually cleanse* you with water, but One is coming—One far more powerful than I, One whose sandals I am not worthy to untie—who will radically purify* you with the Holy Spirit and with fire. ¹⁷He is coming *like a farmer at harvesttime,* tools in hand to separate the wheat from the chaff. He will burn the chaff with unquenchable fire, and He will gather the genuine wheat into His barn.

---

**3:12** Literally, immersion, an act of repentance
**3:16** Literally, immerse

¹⁸He preached with many other provocative figures of speech and so conveyed God's message to the people—*the time had come to re-think everything.* ¹⁹*But John's public preaching ended when* he confronted Herod, the ruler of Galilee, for his many corrupt deeds, including *taking* Herodias, the ruler's sister-in-law, *as his own wife.* ²⁰Herod responded by throwing John into prison.

²¹*But before John's imprisonment, when he was still preaching and* ritually cleansing* the people in the Jordan River, Jesus also came to him to be ritually cleansed. As Jesus prayed, the heavens opened, ²²and the Holy Spirit came upon Him in a physical manifestation that resembled a dove. A voice echoed out from heaven.

**Voice from Heaven** | You are My Son,* the Son I love, and in You I take great pleasure.

*W*hat would it mean for Jesus to be baptized by John? If John's baptism symbolizes a rejection of the religious establishment centered in the temple in Jerusalem, then Jesus' choice to be baptized by John would symbolize that He was aligned with this radical preacher. Jesus wasn't simply coming to strengthen or even renew the centers of power. Instead, He was joining John at the margins to be part of something wild and new that God was doing. And the vivid manifestation of God's pleasure—the dovelike appearance and the voice from heaven— would suggest that even though Jesus was in a sense aligning Himself with John, John was simply the opening act and Jesus was the main attraction. The choreography between John's work and Jesus' work will continue, but from this point on, Jesus is in the center of the story.

---

**3:21** Literally, immersion
**3:22** Psalm 2:7

²³At this, the launch of Jesus' ministry, Jesus was about 30 years old.

He was assumed to be the son of Joseph, the son of Eli, ²⁴the son of Matthat, the son of Levi, the son of Melchi, the son of Jannai, the son of Joseph, ²⁵the son of Mattathias, the son of Amos, the son of Nahum, the son of Hesli, the son of Naggai, ²⁶the son of Maath, the son of Mattathias, the son of Semein, the son of Josech, the son of Joda, ²⁷the son of Joanan, the son of Rhesa, the son of Zerubbabel, the son of Shealtiel, the son of Neri, ²⁸the son of Melchi, the son of Addi, the son of Cosam, the son of Elmadam, the son of Er, ²⁹the son of Joshua, the son of Eliezer, the son of Jorim, the son of Matthat, the son of Levi, ³⁰the son of Simeon, the son of Judah, the son of Joseph, the son of Jonam, the son of Eliakim, ³¹the son of Melea, the son of Menna, the son of Mattatha, the son of Nathan, the son of David, ³²the son of Jesse, the son of Obed, the son of Boaz, the son of Salmon, the son of Nahshon, ³³the son of Amminadab, the son of Admin, the son of Ram, the son of Hezron, the son of Perez, the son of Judah, ³⁴the son of Jacob, the son of Isaac, the son of Abraham, the son of Terah, the son of Nahor, ³⁵the son of Serug, the son of Reu, the son of Peleg, the son of Heber, the son of Shelah, ³⁶the son of Cainan, the son of Arphaxad, the son of Shem, the son of Noah, the son of Lamech, ³⁷the son of Methuselah, the son of Enoch, the son of Jared, the son of Mahalaleel, the son of Cainan, ³⁸the son of Enosh, the son of Seth, the son of Adam, the son of God.

*W*hile genealogies may seem tedious to us, for people in many cultures (including Luke's), genealogies are important and meaningful. They remind us where we come from and give us a sense of identity and history. Luke places Jesus in the mainstream of biblical history, connected to King David, Abraham, Noah, and Adam. Since all humanity is seen as Adam's descendants, Luke shows how Jesus is connected to and relevant for all people. By connecting Jesus with Adam, and ultimately with God, Luke may also be suggesting that in Jesus God is launching a new creation and a new humanity, with Jesus as the new Adam. Unlike the first Adam, though, Jesus will be completely faithful to God, as the next episode will make clear. Perhaps echoing Adam and Eve being tempted by the serpent in the garden,** Luke moves from the stories of Jesus' beginnings to His temptation.

---

**Note Genesis 3:1-7

# Luke 4

## JESUS AND THE DEVIL

¹When Jesus returned from the Jordan River, He was full of the Holy Spirit, and the Holy Spirit led Him away *from the cities and towns* and out into the desert.

²For 40 days, the Spirit led Him from place to place in the desert, and while there, the devil tempted Jesus. Jesus was fasting, eating nothing during this time, and at the end, He was terribly hungry. ³At that point, the devil came to Him.

> **Devil** | Since You're the Son of God, You don't need to be hungry. Just tell this stone to transform itself into bread.

> **Jesus** | ⁴It is written *in the Hebrew Scriptures,* "People need more than bread to live."*

⁵Then the devil gave Jesus a vision. It was as if He traveled around the world in an instant and saw all the kingdoms of the world at once.

> **Devil** | ⁶All these kingdoms, all their glory, I'll give to You. They're mine to give because this whole world has been handed over to me. ⁷If You just worship me, then everything You see will all be Yours. All Yours!

---

4:4 Deuteronomy 8:3

**Jesus** | [8][Get out of My face, Satan!]* The Hebrew
Scriptures say, "Worship and serve the Eternal One
your True God—only Him—and nobody else."*

[9]Then the devil led Jesus to Jerusalem, and he transported Jesus
to stand upon the pinnacle of the temple.

**Devil** | Since You're the Son of God, just jump. Just throw
Yourself into the air. [10]*You keep quoting the Hebrew
Scriptures.* They themselves say,

"He will put His heavenly messengers in charge
of You,
to keep You safe in every way."

[11]And,

"They will hold You up in their hands,
so that You do not smash Your foot against
a stone."*

**Jesus** | [12]*Yes, but* the *Hebrew* Scriptures also say, *"You will not
presume on God; you will not test the True God."**

[13]The devil had no more temptations to offer *that day*, so he left
Jesus, preparing to return at some other opportune time.
[14]Jesus returned to Galilee in the power of the Holy Spirit, and
soon people across the region had heard news of Him. [15]He would

---

**4:8** The oldest manuscripts omit this portion.
**4:8** Deuteronomy 6:13; 10:20
**4:10-11** Psalm 91:11-12
**4:12** Deuteronomy 6:16

regularly go into their synagogues and teach. His teaching earned Him the respect and admiration of everyone who heard Him.

[16]He eventually came to His hometown, Nazareth, and did there what He had done elsewhere *in Galilee*—entered the synagogue and stood up to read *from the Hebrew Scriptures.*

[17]The *synagogue attendant* gave Him the scroll of the prophet Isaiah, and Jesus unrolled it to the place where Isaiah had written these words:

[18]The Spirit of the Lord the Eternal One is on Me.

*Why?* Because the Eternal designated Me

to be His representative to the poor, to preach good news to them.

He sent Me to tell those who are held captive that they can now be set free,

and to tell the blind that they can now see.

He sent Me to liberate those held down by oppression.

[19]*In short, the Spirit is upon Me* to proclaim that now is the time;

This is the jubilee season of the Eternal One's grace.*

*L*uke's original hearers didn't divide the world into sacred/secular, religious/political as we often do. For them, life was integrated. And for them, these words from Isaiah would have a powerful and (in our terminology) *political* meaning: because they saw themselves as oppressed and captivated by the Roman occupation, Jesus' words would suggest that His *good news* described a powerful

---

**4:18-19** Isaiah 61:1-2

change about to come—a change that would liberate the people from their oppression. His fellow Jews had long been waiting for a liberator (or savior) to free them from Roman oppression. Jesus' next words would tell them that their hopes were about to be fulfilled. But then, just as people speak well of Jesus, you'll see how He lets them know that their expectations aren't in line with God's plans. He tells them not to expect God to fit into their boxes and suggests the unthinkable: that God cares for the Gentiles, the very people who are oppressing them! They aren't too pleased by this, as you'll soon see.

²⁰Jesus rolled up the scroll and returned it to the synagogue attendant. Then He sat down, *as a teacher would do,* and all in the synagogue focused their attention on Jesus, *waiting for Him to speak.* ²¹He told them that these words from the Hebrew Scriptures were being fulfilled then and there, in their hearing. *His purpose was to fulfill what Isaiah had described.*

²²At first, everyone was deeply impressed with the gracious words that poured from Jesus' lips. Everyone spoke well of Him and was amazed that He could say these things.

**Everyone** | Wait. This is only the son of Joseph, right?

**Jesus** | ²³You're about to quote the old proverb to Me, "Doctor, heal yourself!" Then you're going to ask Me to prove Myself to you by doing the same miracles I did in Capernaum. ²⁴But face the truth: hometowns always reject their homegrown prophets.

²⁵Think back to the prophet Elijah. There were

many needy Jewish widows in *his homeland*, Israel, when a terrible famine persisted there for three and a half years. ²⁶Yet the only widow God sent Elijah to help was *an outsider*, from Zarephath in Sidon.*

²⁷It was the same with the prophet Elisha. There were many Jewish lepers in his homeland, but the only one he healed—Naaman—*was an outsider* from Syria.*

²⁸The people in the synagogue became furious when He said these things. ²⁹They seized Jesus, took Him to the edge of town, and pushed Him right to the edge of the cliff on which the city was built. They would have pushed Him off and killed Him, ³⁰but He passed through the crowd and went on His way.

³¹⁻³³Next He went to Capernaum, another Galilean city. Again He was *in the synagogue* teaching on the Sabbath, and as before, the people were enthralled by His words. He had a way of saying things—a special authority, *a unique power*.

In attendance that day was a man with a demonic spirit.

**Demon-Possessed Man**
*(screaming at Jesus)*

³⁴*Get out of here!* Leave us alone! What's Your agenda, Jesus of Nazareth? Have You come to destroy us? I know who You are: You're the Holy One, the One sent by God!

**Jesus**
*(firmly rebuking the demon)*

³⁵Be quiet. Get out of that man!

---

**4:26** 1 Kings 17:8-16
**4:27** 2 Kings 5:10-14

Then the demonic spirit immediately threw the man into a fit, and he collapsed right there in the middle of the synagogue. It was clear the demon had come out, and the man was completely fine after that. [36]Everyone was shocked to see this, and they couldn't help but talk about it.

| Synagogue Members | What's this about? What's the meaning of this message? Jesus speaks with authority, and He has power to command demonic spirits to go away. |

[37]The excitement about Jesus spread into every corner of the surrounding region.

[38]*Picture this:*

Jesus then leaves that synagogue and goes over to Simon's place. Simon's mother-in-law is there. She is sick with a high fever. Simon's family asks Jesus to help her.

[39]Jesus stands over her, *and just as He had rebuked the demon,* He rebukes the fever, and the woman's temperature returns to normal. She feels so much better that she gets right up and cooks them all a big meal.

[40]By this time, it's just before nightfall, and as the sun sets, *groups of families, friends, and bystanders come* until a huge crowd has gathered. Each group has brought along family members or friends who are sick with any number of diseases. One by one, Jesus lays His hands on them and heals them. [41]On several occasions, demonic spirits are expelled from these people, after shouting at Jesus, "You are the Son of God!"

Jesus always rebukes them and tells them to be quiet.

They know He is the Liberating King, *but He doesn't want to be acclaimed in this way.*

⁴²The next morning, Jesus sneaks away. He finds a place away from the crowds, but soon they find Him. The crowd tries their best to keep Him from leaving.

**Jesus** | ⁴³No, I cannot stay. I need to preach the kingdom of God to other cities too. This is the purpose I was sent to fulfill.

⁴⁴So He proceeds from synagogue to synagogue across Judea,* preaching His message *of the kingdom of God.*

The essential message of Jesus can be summed up this way: "the kingdom of God is available to everyone, starting now." When Jesus refers to the kingdom of God, He doesn't mean something that happens after we die, far off in heaven; He equates the kingdom of God with God's will being done on earth as it is in heaven. So the kingdom of God is life as God intends it to be—life to the full, life in peace and justice, life in abundance and love. Individuals enter the Kingdom when they enter into a relationship with the Liberating King, when they trust Him enough to follow His ways. But make no mistake, the Kingdom is about more than our individual lives; it is about the transformation and renewal of all God has created. It may start with our individual responses, but it doesn't stop there.

**4:44** Other ancient manuscripts read "Galilee."

Jesus describes His purpose as proclaiming this message. But Jesus not only expresses His message of the kingdom of God in words, He also dramatizes it in deeds. Luke calls these amazing deeds "signs and wonders," suggesting that these actions have symbolic meaning, which is *sign*ificant, and are *wonder*ful, which means they fill people with awe and *wonder*. In the coming chapters, as you encounter these signs and wonders, try to feel the wonder that the original eyewitnesses would have felt, and then ponder their significance as signs of the kingdom of God.

# *Luke 5*

## FISHING FOR PEOPLE

¹*Picture this scene:*

On the banks of Gennesaret Lake, a huge crowd, Jesus in the center of it, presses in to hear His message from God. ²Off to the side, fishermen are washing their nets, leaving their boats unattended on the shore.

³Jesus gets into one of the boats and asks its owner, Simon, to push off *and anchor* a short distance from the beach. Jesus sits down and teaches the people standing on the beach.

⁴After speaking for a while, Jesus speaks to Simon.

> **Jesus** | Move out into deeper water and drop your nets to see what you'll catch.

> **Simon** | ⁵Master, we've been fishing all night, and we
> *(perplexed)* | haven't caught even a minnow. But . . . all right, I'll do it if You say so.

⁶Simon then gets his fellow fishermen to help him let down their nets, *and to their surprise,* the water is bubbling with thrashing fish—*a huge school.* The strands of their nets start snapping under the weight of the catch, ⁷so the crew shouts to the other boat to come out and give them a hand. They start scooping fish out of the nets and into their boats, and before long, their boats are so full of fish they almost sink!

<sup>8-10</sup>Simon's fishing partners, James and John (two of Zebedee's sons), along with the rest of the fishermen, see this incredible haul of fish. They're all stunned, especially Simon. He comes close to Jesus and kneels in front of His knees.

> **Simon** | I can't take this, Lord. I'm a sinful man. You shouldn't be around the likes of me.

> **Jesus** | Don't be afraid, Simon. From now on, I'll ask you to bring Me people instead of fish.

<sup>11</sup>The fishermen haul their fish-heavy boats to land, and they leave everything to follow Jesus.

<sup>12</sup>Another time in a city nearby, a man covered with skin lesions comes along. As soon as he sees Jesus, he prostrates himself.

> **Leper** | Lord, if You wish to, You can heal me of my disease.

<sup>13</sup>Jesus reaches out His hand and touches the man, *something no one would normally do for fear of being infected or of becoming ritually unclean.*

> **Jesus** | I want to heal you. Be cleansed!

Immediately the man is cured. <sup>14</sup>Jesus tells him firmly not to tell anyone about this.

**Jesus** | Go, show yourself to the priest, and do what Moses commanded by making an appropriate offering to celebrate your cleansing. This will prove to everyone what has happened.

¹⁵Even though Jesus said not to talk about what happened, soon every conversation was consumed by these events. The crowds swelled even larger as people went to hear Jesus preach and to be healed of their many afflictions. ¹⁶Jesus repeatedly left the crowds, though, stealing away into the wilderness to pray.

¹⁷One day Jesus was teaching *in a house*, and the healing power of the Lord was with Him. Pharisees and religious scholars were sitting and listening, having come from villages all across the regions of Galilee and Judea and from *the holy city* of Jerusalem.

¹⁸Some men came *to the house*, carrying a paralyzed man on his bed pallet. They wanted to bring him in and present him to Jesus, ¹⁹but the house was so packed with people that they couldn't get in. So they climbed up on the roof and pulled off some roof tiles. Then they lowered the man *by ropes* so he came to rest right in front of Jesus.

²⁰In this way, their faith was visible to Jesus.

**Jesus**
*(to the man
on the pallet)* | My friend, all your sins are forgiven.

²¹The Pharisees and religious scholars were offended at this. They turned to one another and asked questions.

**Pharisees and
Religious
Scholars** | Who does He think He is? Wasn't that blasphemous? Who can pronounce that a person's sins are forgiven? Who but God alone?

**Jesus**
*(responding with His own question)*

<sup>22</sup>Why are your hearts full of questions? <sup>23</sup>Which is easier to say, "Your sins are forgiven," or, "Get up and walk"? <sup>24</sup>Just so you'll know that the Son of Man is fully authorized to forgive sins on earth (He turned to the paralyzed fellow lying on the stretcher), I say, get up, take your mat, and go home.

<sup>25</sup>Then, right in front of their eyes, the man stood up, picked up his bed, and left to go home—full of praises for God! <sup>26</sup>Everyone was stunned. They couldn't help but feel awestruck, and they praised God too.

**People** | We've seen extraordinary things today.

The miracles Jesus performs come in all types. As we've seen, He heals the sick. He frees the oppressed. He shows His power over nature. He will even raise the dead. But as this story shows, one of the greatest miracles of all is forgiveness. To have our sins forgiven—to start over again, to have God separate us from our mistakes and moral failures, to lift the weight of shame and guilt—this may well be the weightiest evidence that the Liberating King is on the move. The kingdom of God doesn't throw all guilty people in jail; it doesn't execute every one of us who have made mistakes or tell us we're just getting what we deserve. Instead, it brings us forgiveness, reconciliation, a new start, a second chance. In this way, it mobilizes us so we can have a new future.

We've seen how Jesus communicates the message of the Kingdom through words and through signs and wonders. Now we'll also see how Jesus embodies the message in the way He treats people, including outcasts like Levi. As a tax collector, Levi is a Jew who works for the Romans, the oppressors, the enemies. No wonder tax collectors were despised! Notice how Jesus treats this compromiser: He doesn't leave him paralyzed in his compromised position; He invites him—like the paralyzed man we just met—to get up and walk, and to walk in a new direction toward a new King and Kingdom.

²⁷Some time later, Jesus walked along the street and saw a tax collector named Levi sitting in his tax office.

**Jesus** | Follow Me.

²⁸And Levi did. He got up from his desk, left everything *(just as the fishermen had)*, and followed Jesus.

²⁹Shortly after this, Levi invited his many friends and associates, including many tax collectors, to his home for a *large* feast in Jesus' honor. Everyone sat at a table together.

*W*hen Jesus healed the paralyzed man, we had our first encounter with a group called the Pharisees. Now they're back again, and they'll be with us through the rest of the story. Pharisaism was a religious movement, consisting of lay people (not clergy) who shared a deep commitment to the Hebrew Scriptures and traditions. They felt that the Jewish people had not yet been liberated from the Romans because of their tolerance of sin. There were too many drunks, too many prostitutes, and too many gluttons. "If we could just get these sinners to change their ways," they felt, "then God would send the One who will liberate us." You can imagine how angry they would be at Jesus for not just forgiving sins (as He did with the paralyzed man) but also for eating with sinners! After all, to eat with someone meant that you loved and accepted them. The kind of Liberator they expected would hate and destroy sinners, not forgive them and enjoy their company!

³⁰The Pharisees and their associates, the religious scholars, got the attention of some of Jesus' disciples.

| Pharisees (in low voices) | *What's wrong with you?* Why are you eating and drinking with tax collectors and other immoral people? |
|---|---|
| Jesus (answering for the disciples) | ³¹Healthy people don't need a doctor, but sick people do. ³²I haven't come for the pure and upstanding; I've come to call *notorious* sinners to rethink their lives and turn to God. |
| Pharisees | ³³Explain to us why You and Your disciples are so commonly found partying like this, when our disciples—and even the disciples of John—are known for fasting rather than feasting, and for saying prayers rather than drinking *wine*. |
| Jesus | ³⁴Imagine there's a wedding going on. Is that the time to tell the guests to ignore the bridegroom |

and fast? [35]Sure, there's a time for fasting—when the bridegroom has been taken away. [36]Look, nobody tears up a new garment to make a patch for an old garment. If he did, the new patch would shrink and rip the old, and the old garment would be worse off than before. [37]And nobody takes freshly squeezed juice and puts it into old, stiff wineskins. If he did, the fresh wine would make the old skins burst open, and both the wine and the wineskins would be ruined. [38]New demands new—new wine for new wineskins. [39]Anyway, those who've never tasted the new wine won't know what they're missing; they'll always say, "The old wine is good enough for me!"

[1-2]One Sabbath Day,* some Pharisees confronted Jesus again. This time, they saw the disciples picking some grain as they walked through the fields. The disciples would dehusk the grain by rubbing the kernels in their hands, and then they would eat it raw.

**Pharisees** | *Don't You know the sacred law says You can't harvest and mill grain* on the Sabbath Day—the day on which all work is forbidden? Why do You think You can ignore the sacred law?

*J*esus, as was His habit, responded to their question with a question of His own. The Pharisees think they have God all figured out. They claim to be experts in the sacred writings—the Scriptures. But Jesus doesn't fit in with their assumptions and expectations, and He doesn't submit to their presumed expertise. So they are constantly criticizing Him and trying to trap Him in some obvious wrongdoing or unorthodoxy. But notice how Jesus responds. He doesn't answer their questions; instead, He asks them questions. He seems to decide that the best way to help them is simply by trying to challenge them to think, to question their assumptions, to open them up to new possibilities, to see things from a higher or deeper perspective. For example, they argue about what is permissible on

---

**6:1** Other manuscripts read "On the second Sabbath after the first."

the Sabbath Day (the seventh day, the day of rest); Jesus gets them
thinking about the deeper purpose of the Sabbath Day, as you'll see
in the next episode.

Jesus | ³*Speaking of the sacred law,* haven't you ever read
about the time when David and his companions
were hungry? ⁴Don't you remember how he went
into the house of God and took the sacred bread of
the presence—which, you may recall, only the
priests were lawfully permitted to eat? Remember
that he not only ate it, but he also gave it to his
companions?* ⁵Likewise, the Son of Man has authority over the Sabbath.

⁶On another Sabbath, Jesus entered the synagogue and taught
there. In the congregation was a man who had a deformed right
hand. ⁷The religious scholars and Pharisees watched Jesus; they sus-
pected that He might try to perform a healing on that day, which
they would use as evidence to convict Him of Sabbath-breaking.

⁸Jesus knew about their plan, and He told the man with the deformed hand to come and stand in front of everyone. The man did
so. ⁹Then Jesus spoke directly to the religious scholars and Pharisees.

Jesus | Here's a question for you: On the Sabbath Day, is it
lawful to do good or to do harm? Is it lawful to save
life or to destroy it?

---

**6:4** 1 Samuel 21:2-6

[10]He turned His gaze to each of them, *one at a time.* Then He spoke to the man.

**Jesus** | Stretch your hand out.

As the man did, his deformed hand was made normal again. [11]This made the Pharisees and religious scholars furious. They began discussing together what they would do to Jesus.

*S*o as you can see, Jesus had His detractors. They watched Him closely and voiced their opposition to His words and actions. Sometimes they would even try to stump Him with questions or publicly humiliate Him. But Jesus refused to be intimidated. For every charge they leveled, He had an answer. To the charge of blasphemy, He responded: "I have the authority to forgive sins." To the charge that He befriended sinners and partied too much, He answered: "These are My people; I've come for them." To the accusation that He broke Sabbath law, He quipped: "The Sabbath is a great servant, but it's not your master. I am Lord of the Sabbath." The crowds were amazed at the tense give-and-take between Jesus and His opponents. They seemed to respect the Pharisees for their strict observance of God's law, or perhaps they feared them because they didn't want to become the target of Pharisaic criticism. Yet they were attracted to Jesus because of the peculiar moral authority He exhibited. As time went on, Jesus crossed more and more lines drawn in the sand. The tension between Jesus and the Pharisees now becomes a major plotline of Luke's story.

¹²Around this time, Jesus went outside the city to a nearby mountain, *along with a large crowd of His disciples.* He prayed through the night to God. ¹³The next morning, He chose 12 of them and gave each a new title—*they were no longer simply disciples, which means "learners";* now they were also *apostles, which means "emissaries."* ¹⁴They included Simon (Jesus called him Peter) and Andrew (Simon's brother); James and John; Philip and Bartholomew; ¹⁵Matthew and Thomas; James (son of Alphaeus) and Simon (known as the Zealot); ¹⁶Judas (son of James), and the other Judas (Judas Iscariot, who later betrayed *Jesus*).

¹⁷The whole crowd of disciples (*including the 12 now designated as emissaries*) came down together, and they stood on a level area nearby. They were joined by an even greater crowd of people who had come from across the whole region—from all of Judea, from Jerusalem, from the coastal areas of Tyre and Sidon. ¹⁸These people came to hear Jesus teach and to be healed by Jesus of their diseases. Those who were troubled by demonic spirits were liberated.

¹⁹Everyone wanted to touch Jesus because when they did, power emanated from Him and they were healed. ²⁰He looked across the faces of His disciples.

> **Jesus** |   All you who are poor, you are blessed
> for the kingdom of God belongs to you.
> ²¹All you who are hungry now, you are blessed
> for your hunger will be satisfied.
> All you who weep now, you are blessed
> for you shall laugh!
> ²²When people hate you,
> when they exclude you and insult you

and write you off as evil on account of the Son
        of Man,
    you are blessed.
²³When these things happen, rejoice! Jump for joy!
        Then you have a great reward in heaven
    For at that moment, you are experiencing
        what the ancient prophets did
        when they were similarly treated
        by the ancestors of your detractors.
²⁴All you who are rich now, you are in danger
        for you have received your comfort in full.
²⁵All you who are full now, you are in danger
        for you shall be hungry.
    All you who laugh now, you are in danger
        for you shall grieve and cry.
²⁶And when everyone speaks well of you,
        you are in danger for their ancestors spoke well
        of the false prophets too.

*E*arlier we met the Pharisees, those who set themselves up as
Jesus' antagonists. Now we've met the disciples, those who place
themselves not against Jesus but with Him, following Him. Here we
have Luke's most concentrated summary of Jesus' teachings for His
followers. Here He describes what life in the kingdom of God looks like.

**Jesus** | ²⁷If you're listening, here's My message: Keep loving
        your enemies no matter what they do. Keep doing

good to those who hate you. [28]Keep speaking blessings on those who curse you. Keep praying for those who mistreat you. [29]If someone strikes you on one cheek, offer the other cheek too. If someone steals your coat, offer him your shirt too. [30]If someone begs from you, give to him. If someone robs you of your valuables, don't demand them back. [31]Think of the kindness you wish others would show you; do the same for them.

[32]Listen, what's the big deal if you love people who already love you? Even scoundrels do that much! [33]So what if you do good to those who do good to you? Even scoundrels do that much! [34]So what if you lend to people who are likely to repay you? Even scoundrels lend to scoundrels if they think they'll be fully repaid.

[35]If you want to be extraordinary—love your enemies! Do good *without restraint*! Lend *with abandon*! Don't expect anything in return! Then you'll receive the truly great reward—you will be children of the Most High—for God is kind to the ungrateful and those who are wicked. [36]So imitate God and be truly compassionate, the way your Father is.

[37]If you don't want to be judged, don't judge. If you don't want to be condemned, don't condemn. If you want to be forgiven, forgive. [38]Don't hold back—give freely, and you'll have plenty poured back into your lap—a good measure, pressed down, shaken together, brimming over. You'll receive in the same measure you give.

<sup>39</sup>Jesus told them this parable:

**Jesus** | What happens if a blind man leads a blind man? Won't both of them fall into a pit? <sup>40</sup>You can't turn out better than your teacher; when you're fully taught, you will resemble your teacher.

<sup>41</sup>Speaking of blindness: Why do you focus on the speck in your brother's eye? Why don't you see the log in your own? <sup>42</sup>How can you say to your brother, "Oh, brother, let me help you take that little speck out of your eye," when you don't even see the big log in your own eye? What a hypocrite! First, take the log out of your own eye. Then you'll be able to see clearly enough to help your brother with the speck in his eye.

<sup>43</sup>*Count on this:* no good tree bears bad fruit, and no bad tree bears good fruit. <sup>44</sup>You can know a tree by the fruit it bears. You don't find figs on a thorn bush, and you can't pick grapes from a briar bush. <sup>45</sup>*It's the same with people.* A person full of goodness in his heart produces good things; a person with an evil reservoir in his heart pours out evil things. The heart overflows in the words a person speaks; your words reveal what's within your heart.

<sup>46</sup>*But it's not just words that matter.* What good is it to mouth the words, "Lord! Lord!" if you don't live by My teachings? <sup>47</sup>What matters is that you come to Me, hear My words, and actually live by them. <sup>48</sup>If you do that, you'll be like the man who wanted to build a sturdy house. He dug down deep and

anchored his foundation to solid rock. During a violent storm, the floodwaters slammed against the house, but they couldn't shake it because of solid craftsmanship. [It was built upon rock.]*

⁴⁹On the other hand, if you hear *My teachings* but don't put them into practice, you'll be like the careless builder who didn't bother to build a foundation under his house. The floodwaters barely touched that pathetic house, and it crashed in ruins in the mud.

As Jesus traveled through Galilee, He taught and healed the crowds in public, but that's not all He did. He also gathered disciples. The word *disciple* means simply a student or an apprentice. So Jesus was the master-teacher, and His disciples were His students. Their classroom was the world—hillsides and beaches, homes and country roads, fields and city streets. Their subject was life—life in the kingdom of God. Jesus had many students, both men and women. But He formed a special inner circle known as "the twelve." The number twelve was highly symbolic because the Jewish people were originally composed of twelve tribes. However, over the centuries some of the tribes had been wiped out. By calling together a new twelve, Jesus seemed to be dramatizing a new beginning for the people of God. The original twelve tribes found their identity in the law of Moses, but now Jesus is giving a new way of life for His twelve to learn and follow.

---

6:48 The oldest manuscripts omit this portion.

## John Has Second Thoughts

¹Jesus shared all these sayings with the crowd that day on the plain. When He was finished, He went into the town of Capernaum. ²There, a Centurion had a slave he loved dearly. The slave was sick— about to die—³so when the Centurion heard about Jesus, he contacted some Jewish elders. He sent them to ask Jesus to come and heal his dear slave. ⁴With great emotion and respect, the elders presented their request to Jesus.

**Jewish Elders** | This man is worthy of Your help. *It's true that he's a Centurion,* ⁵but he loves our nation. In fact, he paid for our synagogue to be built.

⁶So Jesus accompanied them. When they approached the Centurion's home, the Centurion sent out some friends to bring a message to Jesus.

**Message of the Centurion** | Lord, don't go to the trouble of coming inside. I am not worthy to have You come under my roof. ⁷That's why I sent others with my request. Just say the word, and that will be enough to heal my servant. ⁸I understand how authority works, being under authority myself and having soldiers under my authority. I command to one, "Go," and he goes. I say to another, "Come," and he comes. I say to my slave, "Do this," and he obeys me.

⁹Jesus was deeply impressed when He heard this. He turned to the crowd that followed Him.

> **Jesus** | Listen, everyone. *This outsider, this Roman,* has more faith than I have found even among our own Jewish people.

¹⁰The friends of the Centurion returned home, and they found the slave was completely healed.

¹¹It wasn't long after this when Jesus entered a city called Nain. Again all of His disciples accompanied Him, along with a huge crowd. ¹²He was coming near the gate of the city as a corpse was being carried out. This man was the only child *and support* of his widowed mother, and she was accompanied by a large funeral crowd.

¹³As soon as the Lord saw her, He felt compassion for her.

> **Jesus** | Don't weep.

¹⁴Then He came to the stretcher, and those carrying it stood still.

> **Jesus** | Young man, listen! Get up!

¹⁵The dead man immediately sat up and began talking. Jesus presented him to his mother, ¹⁶and everyone was both shocked and jubilant. They praised God.

> **Funeral Crowd** | A tremendous prophet has arisen in our midst! God has visited His people!

¹⁷News of Jesus spread across the whole province of Judea and beyond to the surrounding regions. ¹⁸When these reports reached

John's disciples, they brought news to John himself, *who was known for his preaching and ritual cleansing.*\* ¹⁹John sent two of his disciples to ask the Lord, "Are You the Promised One, or shall we keep looking for someone else?"

²⁰They came to Jesus and asked their question exactly as directed by John.

²¹Before He answered John's messengers, Jesus cured many from various diseases, health conditions, and evil spirits. He even caused many blind people to regain their sight.

| | |
|---|---|
| **Jesus** *(to John's disciples)* | ²²Go and tell John what you've witnessed with your own eyes and ears: the blind are seeing again, the lame are walking again, the lepers are clean again, the deaf hear again, the dead live again, and good news is preached to the poor.\* ²³Whoever is not offended by Me is blessed indeed. |

*J*ohn, it seems, is having second thoughts. Is Jesus really the One we have expected? Is He the Liberating King? But who can blame John for these doubts? After all, John is in prison, unjustly held by a corrupt, immoral ruler. Ultimately, the desert prophet will have his head severed from his body when the drunken, lusty king makes a silly promise in front of dinner guests. So who can blame John for wondering out loud: *Are You the One? Shouldn't John be free to preach, free to ritually cleanse his followers? Shouldn't Jesus be setting up court, fielding an army, and repelling the Roman occupiers?* Jesus,

---

**7:18** Literally, immersion, an act of repentance
**7:22** Isaiah 29:18; 35:5-6

realizing fully the kinds of expectations others had, gently reminds John and his disciples of the Scriptures: "the blind see, the lame walk, the lepers are cleansed, the deaf hear, the dead live, and the poor receive the good news." We don't know how John responded to the report as he neared his own end. What is clear is that Jesus had the utmost respect for His colleague and friend. He didn't reject him for his doubts, but tried to send him reassurance.

²⁴When John's messengers left, Jesus talked to the crowds about John.

Jesus | When you went out into the wilderness to see John, what were you expecting? A reed shaking in the wind? ²⁵What were you looking for? A man in expensive clothing? Look, if you were looking for fancy clothes and luxurious living, you went to the wrong place—you should have gone to the kings' courts, *not to the wilderness!* ²⁶What were you seeking? A prophet? Ah yes, that's what John is, and even more than a prophet. ²⁷*The prophet Malachi* was talking about John when he wrote,

> "I will send My messenger *before You,*
>     to clear Your path in front of You."*

²⁸Listen, there is no human being greater than this man John. Yet even the least significant person in the coming kingdom of God is greater than John.

---

7:27 Malachi 3:1

²⁹*These words elicited two opposite reactions among the people.* The common people and tax collectors heard God's own wisdom in Jesus' assessment of John because they had been ritually cleansed\* by John. ³⁰But the Pharisees and religious scholars hardened their hearts and turned their backs on God's purposes for them because they had refused John's ritual cleansing.

**Jesus** | ³¹The people of this generation—what are they like? To what can they be compared? ³²*I'll tell you:* they're like spoiled kids sitting in the marketplace *playing games,* calling out,

> We played the pipes for you,
> > but you didn't dance to our tune!
> We cried like mourners,
> > but you didn't cry with us!

³³*You can't win with this generation.* John the Preacher comes along, fasting and abstaining from wine, and you say, "This guy is demon-possessed!" ³⁴The Son of Man comes along, feasting and drinking *wine*, and you say, "This guy is a glutton and a drunk, a friend of scoundrels and tax collectors!" ³⁵Well, wisdom's true children know wisdom when they hear it.

³⁶⁻⁴⁰Once a Pharisee named Simon invited Jesus to be a guest for a meal.

*Picture this:*

Just as Jesus enters the man's home and takes His place at the table, a woman from the city—notorious as a woman

---

7:29 Literally, immersed, an act of repentance

of ill repute—follows Him in. She has heard that Jesus will be at the Pharisee's home, so she comes in and approaches Him, carrying an alabaster flask of perfumed oil. Then she begins to cry, she kneels down so her tears fall on Jesus' feet, and she starts wiping His feet with her own hair. Then she actually kisses His feet, and she pours the perfumed oil on them.

**Simon**
*(thinking)* | *Now I know this guy is a fraud.* If He were a real prophet, He would have known this woman is a sinner and He would never let her get near Him, much less touch Him . . . *or kiss Him*!

**Jesus**
*(knowing what the Pharisee is thinking)* | Simon, I want to tell you a story.

**Simon** | Tell me, Teacher.

**Jesus** | ⁴¹Two men owed a certain lender a lot of money. One owed 100 weeks' wages, and the other owed 10 weeks' wages. ⁴²Both men defaulted on their loans, but the lender forgave them both. Here's a question for you: which man will love the lender more?

**Simon** | ⁴³Well, I guess it would be the one who was forgiven more.

**Jesus** | Good answer.

<sup>44-46</sup>Now Jesus turns around so He's facing the woman, although He's still speaking to Simon.

**Jesus** | Do you see this woman here? *It's kind of funny.* I entered your home, and you didn't provide a basin of water so I could wash the road dust from My feet. <sup>45</sup>You didn't give Me a customary kiss of greeting and welcome. You didn't offer Me the common courtesy of providing oil to brighten My face. But this woman has wet My feet with her own tears and washed them with her own hair. She hasn't stopped kissing My feet since I came in. And she has applied perfumed oil to My feet. <sup>47</sup>This woman has been forgiven much, and she is showing much love. But the person who has shown little love shows how little forgiveness he has received.

<sup>48</sup>(to the woman) Your sins are forgiven.

**Simon and Friends**
*(muttering among themselves)* | <sup>49</sup>Who does this guy think He is? He has the audacity to claim the authority to forgive sins?

**Jesus**
*(to the woman)* | <sup>50</sup>Your faith has liberated you. Go in peace.

# Luke 8

¹Soon after this incident, Jesus preached from city to city, village to village, carrying the good news of the kingdom of God. He was accompanied by a group called "the twelve," ²and also by a larger group including some women who had been liberated from evil spirits and healed of diseases. There was Mary, called Magdalene, who had been released from seven demons. ³There were others like Susanna and Joanna, who was married to Chuza, a steward of King Herod. And there were many others too. *These women played an important role in Jesus' ministry,* using their wealth to provide for Him and His other companions.

⁴While a huge crowd gathered with people from many surrounding towns streaming to hear Jesus, He told them a parable.

*W*e've already heard Jesus speak in parables, but in the coming chapters, we'll encounter more and more of these unique teaching devices. Maybe you've never thought of Jesus as an artist, but in a way, parables are works of art, specifically, works of short fiction. They are intricately constructed and complex in their intent. In some ways, they are intended to hide the truth; they don't reduce truth to simple statements or formulae. Instead, they force the reader to take things to a deeper level, to engage the imagination, to think and think again. In this way, they invite people to ask questions; they stir curiosity; they create intrigue. And that's appropriate because Jesus' message of the kingdom of God is nothing if it's not intriguing!

**Jesus** | [5]Once a farmer went out to scatter seed *in his fields.*
Some seeds fell along a trail where they were
crushed underfoot by people walking by. Birds flew
in and ate those seeds. [6]Other seeds fell on gravel.
Those seeds sprouted but soon withered, depleted
of moisture *under the scorching sun.* [7]Still other seeds
landed among thorns where they grew for a while,
but eventually the thorns stunted them so they
couldn't thrive or bear fruit. [8]But some seeds fell
into good soil—*soft, moist, free from thorns.* These
seeds not only grew, but they also produced *more
seeds,* a hundred times what the farmer originally
planted. If you have ears, hear My meaning!

[9]His disciples heard the words, but the deeper meaning eluded
them.

**Disciples** | What were You trying to say?

**Jesus** | [10]The kingdom of God contains many secrets.
They keep listening, but do not comprehend;
keep observing, but do not understand.*
I want you to understand, so [11]here's the inter-
pretation: The voice of God falls on human hearts
like seeds scattered across a field. [12]Some people
hear that message, but the devil opposes the liberation that would come to them by believing. So he
swoops in and steals the message from their hard

8:10 Isaiah 6:9

hearts like birds stealing the seeds from the foot-path. [13]Others receive the message enthusiastically, but their vitality is short-lived because the message cannot be deeply rooted in their shallow hearts. In the heat of temptation, their faith withers, like the seeds that sprouted in gravelly soil. [14]A third group hears the message, but as time passes the daily anxieties, the pursuit of wealth, and life's addicting delights outpace the growth of the message in their hearts. Even if the message blossoms and fruit begins to form, the fruit never fully matures because the thorns choke out the plants' vitality.

[15]But some people hear the message and let it take root deeply in receptive hearts made fertile by honesty and goodness. With patient dependability, they bear good fruit.

[16]If you light a lamp, you're not going to cover it with a clay pot. You're not going to hide it under your bed. If you light a lamp, you're going to put it out in the open so your guests *can feel welcome and* see where they're going.

[17]Hidden things will always come out into the open. Secret things will come to light and be exposed. [18]*I hope you're still listening.* And I hope you're listening carefully. If you get what I'm saying, you'll get more. If you miss My meaning, even the understanding you think you have will be taken from you.

[19]Around this time, Jesus was speaking to a crowd of people gathered in a house. His mother and brothers arrived to see Him, but the

crowd around Him was so huge that they couldn't even get through the door. [20]Word spread through the crowd.

**Someone from the Crowd** | Jesus, Your mother and brothers are outside the house hoping to see You.

**Jesus** | [21]Do you want to know who My mother and brothers are? They're the ones who truly understand God's message and obey it.

[22]*Picture this:* One day Jesus and His disciples get into a boat.

**Jesus** | Let's cross the lake.

So they push off from shore and begin sailing to the far side. [23]As they progress across the lake, Jesus falls sound asleep. Soon a raging storm blows in. The waves wash over the sides of the boat, and the boat starts filling up with water. Every second the situation becomes more dangerous.
[24]The disciples *shake Jesus* and wake Him.

**Disciples**
*(shouting)* | Master! Master! We're all going to die!

Jesus wakes up and tells the wind to stop whipping them around, and He tells the furious waves to calm down. They do just that. [25]Then Jesus turns to the disciples.

**Jesus** | What happened to your faith?

The disciples had been terrified during the storm, but now they're afraid in another way. They turn to each other and start whispering, chattering, and wondering.

**Disciples** | Who is this man? How can He command wind and water so they do what He says?

²⁶When they get to the other side of the lake, in the Gerasene country opposite Galilee, ²⁷a man from the city is waiting for Jesus when He steps out of the boat. The man is full of demonic spirits. He's been running around for a long time stark naked, and he's homeless, sleeping among the dead in a cemetery. ²⁸⁻²⁹This man has on many occasions been tied up and chained and kept under guard, but each time he has broken free and the demonic power has driven him back into remote places *away from human contact*. Jesus commands the demonic force to leave him. The man looks at Jesus and starts screaming. He falls down in front of Jesus.

**Possessed Man** *(shouting)* | Don't torment me, Jesus, Son of the Most High God! Why are You here?

**Jesus** *(calmly and simply)* | ³⁰What's your name?

**Possessed Man** | Battalion.

He says this because an army of demons is inside of him. ³¹The demons start begging Jesus not to send them into the bottomless pit. ³²They plead instead to enter into a herd of pigs feeding on a steep hillside near the shore. Jesus gives them permission to do so. ³³Suddenly the man is liberated from the demons, but the pigs—they stampede, squealing down the hill and into the lake where they drown themselves.

³⁴The pig owners see all this. They run back to their town and tell everyone in the region about it. ³⁵Soon a crowd rushes from the town to see what's going on out by the lake. There they find Jesus seated *to teach* with the newly liberated man sitting at His feet *learning in the posture of a disciple*. This former madman is now properly dressed and completely sane. This frightens the people. ³⁶The pig owners tell them the whole story—the healing, *the pigs' mass suicide, everything*.

³⁷The people are scared to death, and they don't want this scary abnormality happening in their territory. They ask Jesus to leave immediately. *Jesus doesn't argue.* He prepares to leave, ³⁸but before they embark, the newly liberated man begs to come along and join the band of disciples.

> **Jesus** | ³⁹No. Go home. Tell your people this amazing story about how much God has done for you.

The man does so. In fact, he tells everyone in the whole city how much Jesus did for him that day *on the shore*.

⁴⁰When Jesus and His disciples crossed the lake, another crowd was waiting to welcome Him. ⁴¹A man made his way through the crowd. His name was Jairus, and he was a synagogue official. *Like the man on the other side of the lake,* this dignified man also fell at Jesus'

feet, begging Jesus to visit his home ⁴²where his only daughter, a girl of 12, lay dying. Jesus set out with Jairus. The crowd came along too, pressing hard against Him.

⁴³In the crowd was a woman. She had suffered from an incurable menstrual disorder for 12 years [and had spent her livelihood on doctors with no effect].* *It had kept her miserable and ritually unclean, unable to participate in Jewish life.* ⁴⁴*She followed Jesus, working her way through the crowd closer to Him* until she could reach Him. She touched the fringe of the robe Jesus wore, and at that moment the bleeding stopped.

| | |
|---|---|
| **Jesus**<br>*(stopping and looking about)* | ⁴⁵Who touched Me? |
| **Crowd**<br>*(everyone speaking at once)* | Not me. It wasn't me either. |
| **Peter [and those with him]***<br>*(intervening)* | Master, what kind of question is that, with this huge crowd all around You and many people touching You on all sides? |
| **Jesus** | ⁴⁶*I felt something.* I felt power going out from Me. I know that somebody touched Me. |

⁴⁷The woman now realized her secret was going to come out sooner or later, so she stepped out of the crowd, shaking with fear, and she fell down in front of Jesus. Then she told her story in front of everyone—why she touched Him, what happened as a result.

---

**8:43** This portion is omitted in some ancient manuscripts.
**8:45** The earliest manuscripts omit this portion.

**Jesus** | ⁴⁸Your faith has made you well again, daughter. Go in peace.

⁴⁹Right at that instant, one of *Jairus's* household servants arrived.

**Servant** | Sir, your daughter is dead. It's no use bothering the Teacher with this anymore.

**Jesus**
*(interrupting Jairus before he could speak)* | ⁵⁰Don't be afraid. Just believe. She'll be well again.

⁵¹⁻⁵²As they approached the house, the whole neighborhood was full of the sound of mourning—weeping, wailing, loud crying. Jesus told everyone to stay outside—everyone except Peter, John, James, and, of course, the girl's father and mother.

**Jesus**
*(to the mourners)* | Please stop weeping. The girl isn't dead. She's only asleep.

⁵³They knew for certain that she was dead, *so their bitter tears now mixed* with mocking laughter *at what they thought was the naïveté or stupidity of Jesus' remark.*

⁵⁴Meanwhile, inside, Jesus took the girl's hand.

**Jesus** | Child, get up!

⁵⁵She started breathing again, and she sat right up.

**Jesus** | Get her something to eat.

⁵⁶Her parents were amazed, but Jesus sternly told them to keep what had happened a secret.

*W*e've just completed an almost breathtaking succession of encounters between Jesus and people in need. Each story is unique; Jesus responds to each person as an individual, and there is no detectable formula to His way of treating people—except that in every case, His interactions are characterized by love and compassion. But now Jesus takes His ministry of teaching the kingdom of God in word and deed to a new level: He sends out His disciples to do what they have seen Him do. Jesus commissions the twelve to multiply His ministry. So in the coming episodes, we see them go out from and then return to report to Jesus what they've experienced and learned. But as you'll see, it's hard for them to get any time alone to talk. There are so many people who want time with Jesus!

## SPEECHLESS AND STUNNED

¹Jesus convened a gathering of the twelve. He gave them power and authority to free people from all demonic spirits and to heal them of diseases. ²He sent them out to preach the kingdom of God and to heal the sick. These were His instructions:

³1. Travel light on your journey: don't take a staff, backpack, bread, money, or even an extra change of clothes.

⁴2. When you enter a house, stay there until you leave that city.

⁵3. If a town rejects you, shake the dust from your feet as you leave as a witness against them.

⁶The disciples left on their journeys from village to village. They preached the good news, and they healed the sick everywhere they went.

⁷⁻⁸*Their mission didn't go unnoticed.* The local official installed by Rome, Herod, was especially anxious about the news because rumors were flying *that something unprecedented was occurring.* Some people said that Elijah or one of the other ancient prophets had been resurrected, while others said that John, *famous for his ritual cleansing,** was alive *and preaching again.*

**Herod** | ⁹I am the one who beheaded John. So who is this man who is causing such a stir?

Herod *was curious about Jesus and* wanted to see Him.

---

**9:7-8** Literally, immersion, an act of repentance

[10]The emissaries whom Jesus had sent out returned, and Jesus took them away from the crowds for a time of retreat in a city called Bethsaida. They gave Jesus a full report of their accomplishments and experiences. [11]But soon the crowds discovered where they were and pursued Him. Jesus didn't turn them away; He welcomed them, spoke of the kingdom of God to them, and brought health to those who needed healing.

[12]*Picture what happened* while in Bethsaida, where Jesus and His disciples were spending time with the crowds:

> The sun is low in the sky, and soon it will be dusk. The twelve come to Jesus with advice.

Disciples | Send the crowd away so they can find lodging and food in the nearby villages and country-side. We're out here in the middle of nowhere.

Jesus | [13-14]No. You give them something to eat.

Disciples | *Are You kidding?* There are at least 5,000 men here, *not to mention women and children.* All we have are five loaves and two fish. The only way we could provide for them would be to go to a nearby city and buy cartloads of food. *That would cost a small fortune.*

Jesus | Just do this: organize them in little communities of about 50 people each and have them sit down.

¹⁵They do what Jesus says, and soon groups of 50 are scattered across the landscape.

¹⁶Then Jesus takes the five loaves and two fish, and He looks up to heaven. He praises God for the food, takes each item, and breaks it into fragments. Then He gives fragments to the twelve disciples and tells them to distribute the food to the crowd.

¹⁷Everyone eats. Everyone is satisfied. Nobody goes away hungry. In fact, when the disciples recover the leftovers, they have 12 baskets full of broken pieces.

¹⁸Once, Jesus was praying in solitude. The disciples were nearby, and He came to them with a question.

Jesus | What are the people saying about Me?

Disciples | ¹⁹Some people think You're John the Preacher. Others say You're the prophet Elijah, or else one of the other ancient prophets who has come back from the dead.

Jesus | ²⁰Ah, but what about you? Who do you say that I am?

Peter | You are the Liberating King sent by God.

Jesus (sternly) | ²¹Don't tell anyone this. ²²The Son of Man must suffer intensely. He must be rejected by the religious establishment—the elders, the chief priests, the religious scholars. Then He will be killed. And then, on the third day He will be raised.

²³If any of you want to walk My path, you're going to have to deny yourself. You'll have to take up your cross every day and follow Me. ²⁴If you try to avoid danger and risk, then you'll lose everything. If you let go of your life and risk all for My sake, then your life will be liberated, *healed, made whole and full.* ²⁵Listen, what good does it do you if you gain everything—if the whole world is in your pocket—but then your own life slips through your fingers and is lost to you?

²⁶If you're ashamed of who I am and what I teach, then the Son of Man will be ashamed of you when He comes in all His glory, the glory of the Father, and the glory of the holy angels. ²⁷*Are you ready for this?* I'm telling you the truth: some of you will not taste death until your eyes see the kingdom of God.

*I*n this section of Luke, Jesus is working hard with the disciples. They have a lot to learn and not much time left to learn it. But their "not-getting-it-factor" is quite amazing at times. We can almost see Luke shaking his head and chuckling as he writes, thinking about how foolish the disciples can be at times. And of course, he's probably thinking of himself too . . . just as we do when we read about the stupid things the disciples say and do—one moment seeing and hearing glorious things, the next moment missing the point entirely.

²⁸Those words had about eight days *to settle in with the disciples.* Then, once again, Jesus went away to pray. This time He took along

only Peter, John, and James. They climbed a mountainside *and came to a place of solitude.*

²⁹⁻³²Jesus began to pray and the disciples tried to stay awake, but their eyes grew heavier and heavier and finally they all fell asleep. When they awakened, they looked over at Jesus and saw something inexplicable happening. Jesus was changing before their eyes, beginning with His face. It seemed to glow. The glow spread, and even His clothing took on a blinding whiteness. Then, two figures appeared in the glorious radiance emanating from Jesus. The three disciples somehow knew that these figures were Moses and Elijah. Peter, James, and John overheard the conversation that took place between Jesus, Moses, and Elijah—a conversation that centered on Jesus' "departure," and how He would accomplish this departure from the capital city, Jerusalem.

³³*The glow began to fade, and* it was clear that Moses and Elijah were about to disappear.

**Peter**
*(to Jesus)* | Please, Master, it is good for us to be here *and see this.* Can we make three structures, one to honor You, one to honor Moses, and one to honor Elijah, *to try to capture what's happening here?*

Peter had no idea what he was saying.

³⁴While he spoke a cloud descended, and they were enveloped in it, and fear fell on them. ³⁵Then a voice came out of everywhere and nowhere at once.

**Voice from Heaven** | This is My Son!* This is the One I have chosen! Listen to Him!

---

**9:35** Psalm 2:7; Luke 3:22

³⁶Then the voice was silent, *the cloud disappeared,* and Moses and Elijah were gone. Peter, James, and John were left speechless, *stunned, staring at* Jesus who now stood before them alone. For a long time, they did not say a word about this whole experience.

³⁷They came down the mountain, and the next day yet another huge crowd gathered around Jesus. There was a man in the crowd who shouted out.

**Man in Crowd** | ³⁸Teacher! Please come look at my son here, my only child. ³⁹From time to time, a demonic spirit seizes him. It makes him scream and go into convulsions. He foams at the mouth. It nearly destroys him and only leaves after causing him great distress. ⁴⁰*While You were up on the mountain,* I begged Your disciples to liberate him from this spirit, but they were incapable of helping us.

**Jesus** | ⁴¹O generation faithless, twisted, and crooked, how long can I be with you? How much can I bear? Bring your boy here.

⁴²The boy had taken a few steps toward Jesus when suddenly the demon seemed to rip into the boy, throwing him into convulsions. Jesus spoke sternly to the demonic spirit, and the boy was healed. Jesus presented the boy to his father.

⁴³*The crowd began cheering and* discussing this amazing healing and the power of God, but Jesus turned to His disciples.

**Jesus** | ⁴⁴Listen. Listen hard. Let these words get down

deep: the Son of Man is going to be turned over to
the authorities and arrested.

⁴⁵They had no idea what He meant by this; they heard the words
but missed the meaning, and they felt too afraid to ask Him to explain further.

⁴⁶Later the close followers of Jesus began to argue over *the stupid
and vain* question, "Which one of us is the greatest disciple?"

⁴⁷Jesus saw what was going on—*not just the argument, but* the
deeper heart issues, so He found a child and had the child stand beside Him.

Jesus | ⁴⁸*See this little one?* Whoever welcomes a little child in
My name welcomes Me. And whoever welcomes Me
welcomes the One who sent Me. The smallest one
among you is therefore the greatest.

John | ⁴⁹Master, we found this fellow casting out demons.
He said he was doing it in Your name, but he's not
one of our group. So we told him to stop.

Jesus | ⁵⁰*What?* No! Don't think like that! Whoever is not
working against you is working with you.

⁵¹The time approached for Him to be taken back up *to the Father*;
so strong with resolve, Jesus made Jerusalem His destination.

⁵²He sent some people ahead of Him into the territory of the
Samaritans, *a minority group at odds with the Jewish majority.* He wanted
His messengers to find a place for them to stay in a village *along the*

*road to Jerusalem.* ⁵³But because the Samaritans realized Jesus was going to Jerusalem, they refused to welcome them. ⁵⁴*James and John were
outraged.*

**James and**   |   Lord, do You want us to call down fire from heaven
**John**   |   to destroy these people who have rejected You?*
[Just as Elijah did.]*

**Jesus**   |   ⁵⁵You just don't get it. ⁵⁶[The Son of Man didn't
*(turning toward*   |   come to ruin the lives of people, but He came to
*them and shaking*   |   liberate them.]*
*His head)*

He led them on toward another village. ⁵⁷Farther along on the
road, a man volunteered to become a disciple.

**Volunteer**   |   I'll follow You to any destination.

**Jesus**   |   ⁵⁸Foxes are at home in their burrows. Birds are at
home in their nests. But the Son of Man has no
home. ⁵⁹You (to another person)—I want you to follow Me!

**Another**   |   *I'd be glad to,* Teacher, but let me first attend to my
**Volunteer**   |   father's funeral.

**Jesus**   |   ⁶⁰Let the dead bury their dead. I'm giving you a dif-
ferent calling—to go and proclaim the kingdom of
God.

---

**9:54** 2 Kings 1:10,12
**9:54** Most ancient manuscripts omit this portion.
**9:56** The earliest manuscripts omit this portion of verse 56.

| | |
|---|---|
| **A Third Volunteer** | [61]I'll come, Jesus. I'll follow You. But just let me first run home to say good-bye to my family. |
| **Jesus** | [62]Listen, if your hand is on the plow but your eyes are looking backwards, then you're not fit for the kingdom of God. |

# Luke 10

## GO BAREFOOT AND QUIETLY

¹The Lord then recruited and deployed 70* more disciples. He sent them ahead, in teams of two, to visit all the towns and settlements between them and Jerusalem. ²This is what He ordered.

**Jesus** | There's a great harvest waiting in the fields, but there aren't many good workers to harvest it. Pray that the Harvest Master will send out good workers to the fields.

³It's time for you 70 to go. I'm sending you out *armed with vulnerability*, like lambs walking into a pack of wolves. ⁴Don't bring a wallet. Don't carry a backpack. I don't even want you to wear sandals. Walk along *barefoot, quietly*, without stopping for small talk. ⁵When you enter a house seeking lodging, say, "Peace on this house!" ⁶If a child of peace—one who welcomes God's message of peace—is there, your peace will rest on him. If not, don't worry; nothing is wasted. ⁷Stay where you're welcomed. *Become part of the family*, eating and drinking whatever they give you. You're My workers, and you deserve to be cared for. Again, don't go from house to house, ⁸but settle down in a town and eat whatever they serve you. ⁹Heal the sick and say to the townspeople, "The kingdom of God has come near to you."

---

10:1 Other ancient manuscripts read "72."

¹⁰Of course, not every town will welcome you. If you're rejected, walk through the streets and say, ¹¹*"We're leaving this town.* We'll wipe off the dust that clings to our feet in protest against you. But even so, know this: the kingdom of God has come near." ¹²I tell you the truth, on *judgment* day, Sodom will have an easier time of it than the town *that rejects My messengers.*

¹³It's going to be bad for you, Chorazin! It's going to be bad for you, Bethsaida! If the mighty works done in your streets had been done in the cities of Tyre and Sidon, they would have been moved to turn to God and cry out in sackcloth and ashes. ¹⁴On judgment day, Tyre and Sidon will have an easier time of it than you. ¹⁵It's going to be bad for you too, Capernaum! Will you be celebrated to heaven? No, you will go down to the place of the dead.

¹⁶*Listen, disciples:* if people give you a hearing, they're giving Me a hearing. If they reject you, they're rejecting Me. And if they reject Me, they're rejecting the One who sent Me. *So—go now!*

¹⁷When the 70* *completed their mission and* returned *to report on their experiences,* they were elated.

> **Seventy** | It's amazing, Lord! When we use Your name, the demons do what we say!

---

**10:17** Other ancient manuscripts read "72."

Jesus | [18]*I know. I saw it happening.* I saw Satan falling from above like a lightning bolt. [19]I've given you true authority. You can smash vipers and scorpions under your feet.* You can walk all over the power of the enemy. You can't be harmed. [20]But listen—that's not the point. Don't be elated that evil spirits leave when you say to leave. Rejoice that your names are written in heaven.

[21]Then Jesus Himself became elated. The Holy Spirit was on Him, and He began to pray with joy.

Jesus | Thank You, Father, Lord of heaven and earth. Thank You for hiding Your mysteries from the wise and intellectual, instead revealing them to little children. Your ways are truly gracious. [22]My Father has given Me everything. No one knows the full identity of the Son except the Father, and nobody knows the full identity of the Father except the Son, and the Son fully reveals the Father to whomever He wishes. [23](then almost in a whisper to the disciples) How blessed are your eyes to see what you see! [24]Many prophets and kings dreamed of seeing what you see, but they never got a glimpse. They dreamed of hearing what you hear, but they never heard it.

[25]Just then a scholar *of the Hebrew Scriptures* tried to trap Jesus, *to make Him look stupid.*

**10:19** Psalm 91:13

**Scholar** | Teacher, what must I do to experience the eternal life?

**Jesus**
*(answering with a question)* | ²⁶What is written in the *Hebrew* Scriptures? How do you interpret their answer to your question?

**Scholar** | ²⁷You shall love—"love the Eternal One your True God with everything you have: all your heart, all your soul, all your strength, and all your mind"*— and "love your neighbor as yourself."*

**Jesus** | ²⁸*Perfect.* Your answer is correct. Follow these commands and you will live.

²⁹The scholar *was frustrated by this response because he* was hoping to make himself appear smarter than Jesus.

**Scholar** | Ah, but who is my neighbor?

**Jesus** | ³⁰This fellow was traveling down from Jerusalem to Jericho when some robbers mugged him. They took his clothes, beat him to a pulp, and left him naked and bleeding and in critical condition. ³¹By chance, a priest was going down that same road, and when he saw the wounded man, he crossed over to the other side and passed by. ³²Then a Levite *who was on his way to assist in the temple* also came and saw the victim lying there, and he too kept his distance.

---

**10:27** Deuteronomy 6:5
**10:27** Leviticus 19:18

³³Then a *despised* Samaritan journeyed by. When he saw the fellow, he felt compassion for him. ³⁴The Samaritan went over to him, stopped the bleeding, applied some first aid, and put the poor fellow on his donkey. He brought the man to an inn and cared for him through the night.

³⁵The next day, the Samaritan took out some money—two days' wages to be exact*—and paid the innkeeper, saying, "Please take care of this fellow, and if this isn't enough, I'll repay you next time I pass through."

³⁶Which of these three proved himself a neighbor to the man who had been mugged by the robbers?

**Scholar** | ³⁷The one who showed mercy to him.

**Jesus** | Well then, go and behave like that Samaritan.

*T*his story brings together many themes from Jesus' teaching of the Kingdom. Samaritans in Jesus' day were seen as "half-breeds" by Jesus' fellow Jews—racially mixed and also religiously compromised. By making a Samaritan the hero of the story, Jesus is once again tweaking assumptions and breaking out of conventional boxes: "In the kingdom of God," Jesus is saying, "the outcasts and last can move to the front of the line." The focus for Jesus is not on the kinds

---

10:35 Roman coin denarii

of sophisticated arguments preferred by the religious scholar; for Jesus, the kingdom of God is about living life, and in particular, living a life of love for God and for neighbor—whoever that neighbor may be.

[38]Jesus continued from there *toward Jerusalem* and came to another village. Martha, a resident of that village, welcomed Jesus into her home. [39]Her sister, Mary, went and sat at Jesus' feet, listening to Him teach. [40]Meanwhile, Martha was anxious about all the hospitality arrangements.

**Martha**
*(interrupting Jesus)* | Lord, why don't You care that my sister is leaving me to do all the work by myself? Tell her to get over here and help me.

**Jesus** | [41]Oh Martha, Martha, you are so anxious and concerned about a million details, [42]but really, only one thing matters. Mary has chosen that one thing, and I won't take it away from her.

# Luke 11

## CHOOSING SIDES

¹Another time Jesus was praying, and when He finished, one of His disciples approached Him.

**Disciple** | Teacher, would You teach us Your way of prayer? John taught his disciples his way of prayer, *and we're hoping You'll do the same.*

**Jesus** | ²Here's how to pray:

Father [in heaven], may Your name be revered.
  May Your kingdom come.
[Your will be accomplished on earth
    as it is in heaven.]
³Give us the food we need for tomorrow,
⁴And forgive us for our wrongs,
  for we forgive those who wrong us.
And lead us away from temptation.
  [And save us from the evil one.]*

⁵Imagine that one of your friends comes over at midnight. He bangs on the door and shouts, "Friend, will you lend me three loaves of bread?

---

**11:2-4** The earliest manuscripts omit the bracketed text.

⁶A friend of mine just showed up unexpectedly from a journey, and I don't have anything to feed him." ⁷Would you shout out from your bed, "I'm already in bed, and so are the kids. I already locked the door. I can't be bothered"? ⁸You know this as well as I do: even if you didn't care that this fellow was your friend, if he keeps knocking long enough, you'll get up and give him whatever he needs simply because of his brash persistence!

⁹So listen: Keep on asking, and you will receive. Keep on seeking, and you will find. Keep on knocking, and the door will be opened for you. ¹⁰All who keep asking will receive, all who keep seeking will find, and doors will open to those who keep knocking.

¹¹Some of you are fathers, so ask yourselves this: if your son comes up to you and asks for a fish for dinner, will you give him a snake instead? ¹²If your boy wants an egg to eat, will you give him a scorpion? ¹³Look, all of you are flawed in so many ways, yet in spite of all your faults, you know how to give good gifts to your children. How much more will your Father in heaven give the Holy Spirit to all who ask!

¹⁴*Picture this:*

Jesus is exorcising a demon that has long kept a man from speaking. When the demon is expelled, the man starts talking and the people are amazed. ¹⁵*But then controversy erupts.*

**Some People** | Do you know why He can cast out demons? It's because He's in league with the demon prince, Beelzebul.

¹⁶Other people want to see more, so they challenge Jesus to give them another miraculous sign. ¹⁷Jesus knows what they're thinking.

**Jesus** | *People, be logical.* If a kingdom is divided against itself, it will collapse. If a ruling family is divided against itself, it will fall apart.

¹⁸So if Satan's kingdom is divided against itself, won't his whole enterprise collapse? Does it make any sense to say I'm casting out demons by Beelzebul? ¹⁹Besides, if you're saying it takes satanic power to cast out Satan, by whose power do your own exorcists work? If you condemn Me for an exorcism, you'll have to condemn them; *do you really want to do that?* ²⁰But if I by the power of God cast out demonic spirits, then *face this fact*: the kingdom of God is here, *just as I've been saying.*

²¹When a man of power with his full array of weapons guards his own palace, everything inside is secure. ²²But when a new man who is stronger and better armed attacks the palace, the old ruler will be

overcome, his weapons and trusted defenses will be removed, and his treasures will be plundered. *Can you see Satan as that old man of power and Me as the new man of power?* [23]Can you see that I'm asking you to choose whose side you're on—working with Me or fighting against Me?

[24]*You seem to think you're experts on demonic spirits, but let Me instruct you:* When a demonic spirit is expelled from someone, he wanders through waterless wastelands seeking rest. But there is no rest for him anywhere, so he says, "I'm going back to my old house." [25]He returns and finds the old house has been swept clean and fixed up again. [26]So he goes and finds seven other spirits even worse than he is, and they make themselves at home in the man's life so that he's worse off now than he was before.

[27]As He is speaking, a woman shouts out from the crowd and interrupts Him.

Woman | How blessed is Your mother's womb for bearing You! How blessed are her [28]breasts for nursing You!

Jesus | No, how blessed are those who hear God's voice and make God's message their way of life.

²⁹*Jesus was becoming more and more popular,* and the crowds swelled wherever He went. *He wasn't impressed.*

Jesus | This generation is evil. These people are seeking signs *and spectacles, but I'm not going to play their game.* The only sign they will be given is the sign of Jonah. ³⁰Just as Jonah became a sign to the people of Nineveh, so will the Son of Man be to this generation.

³¹The queen of Ethiopia will stand to condemn the people of this generation on the day of judgment. She, *an outsider,* came from so far away to hear the wisdom given to Solomon, but now, something greater than Solomon is here: *how are the people of this generation responding?*

³²Similarly, the people of Nineveh will stand to condemn the people of this generation on the day of judgment. They, *outsiders,* responded and changed because of the preaching of Jonah, but now, something greater than Jonah is here: *how are the people of this generation responding?*

³³*You need a light to see.* Only an idiot would light a lamp and then put it beneath the floor or under a bucket. No, any intelligent person would put the lamp on a table so everyone who comes in the house can see. ³⁴Listen, your eye, *your outlook, the way you see*—is your lamp. If your way of seeing is functioning well, then your whole life will be enlightened. But if your way of seeing is darkened, then your life

will be a dark, dark place. ³⁵So be careful, people, because your light may be malfunctioning. ³⁶If your outlook is good, then your whole life will be bright, with no shadowy corners, as when a radiant lamp brightens your home.

*I*n the next several episodes, Jesus engages in tense conversation with the Pharisees and other religious scholars. Jesus is fearless in His engagement with them. But the series of episodes begins with Jesus agreeing to eat in the home of a Pharisee where a religious scholar has also been invited—a sign that underneath their conflict, Jesus loved them and wanted to get through to them.

³⁷A Pharisee interrupted His speech with an invitation to dinner. Jesus accepted the invitation and took His place at his table. ³⁸The Pharisee was offended that Jesus didn't perform the ceremonial hand-washing before eating—*something Pharisees were fastidious about doing.*

Jesus | ³⁹You Pharisees *are a walking contradiction.* You are so concerned about external things—like someone who washes the outside of a cup and bowl, but never cleans the inside, *which is what counts!* Beneath your fastidious exterior is a mess of extortion and filth.

⁴⁰You guys don't get it. Did the potter make the outside but not the inside too? ⁴¹*If you were full of*

*goodness within,* you could overflow with generosity from within, and if you did that, everything would be clean for you.

⁴²Woe to you, Pharisees! *Judgment will come on you!* You are fastidious about tithing—keeping account of every little leaf of mint and herb, but you neglect what really matters: justice and the love of God! If you'd get straight on what really matters, then your fastidiousness about little things would be worth something.

⁴³Woe to you, Pharisees! *Judgment will come on you!* What you really love is having people fawn over you when you take the seat of honor in the synagogue or when you are greeted in the public market.

⁴⁴*Wake up! See what you've become!* Woe to you; you're like a field full of unmarked graves. People walk on the field and have no idea of the corruption that's a few inches beneath their feet.

| | |
|---|---|
| **Scholar**<br>*(sitting at Jesus'*<br>*table)* | ⁴⁵Rabbi, if You insult the Pharisees, then You insult us too. |
| **Jesus** | ⁴⁶Well, *now that you mention it,* watch out, all you religious scholars! *Judgment will come on you too!* You load other people down with unbearable burdens *of rules and regulations,* but you don't lift a finger to help others. ⁴⁷⁻⁴⁸Woe to you; *you don't fool anybody! You seem very religious*—honoring the prophets by building them elaborate memorial tombs. Come to think of |

it, that's very fitting, since you're so much like the people who killed the prophets! They killed the prophets, you build their tombs—*you're all in the same family business!*

⁴⁹This is why the Wisdom of God said, "I will send these people prophets and emissaries, and these people will kill and persecute many of them." ⁵⁰As a result, this generation will be held accountable for the blood of all the prophets shed from the very beginning of time, ⁵¹from Abel's blood to Zechariah's blood, who was killed in the temple itself between the altar and the holy place. I'm serious: this generation will be held accountable.

⁵²So, religious scholars, judgment will come on you! *Don't think you'll evade the consequences of your behavior. You're supposed to be teachers, unlocking the doorway of knowledge and guiding people through it.* But the fact is, you've never even passed through the doorway yourselves. You've taken the key, left the door locked tight, and stood in the way of everyone who sought entry.

⁵³After that dinner, things were never the same. The religious scholars and Pharisees put constant pressure on Jesus, ⁵⁴trying to trap Him and trick Him into saying things they could use to bring Him down.

# *Luke 12*

## Excuse Me, Mr. Brilliant

¹The crowds at this time were packed in so tightly that thousands of people were stepping on each other. Jesus spoke to His disciples, *knowing that the crowds could overhear.*

**Jesus** | Guard yourselves from the yeast that puffs up the Pharisees—hypocrisy, *false appearance, trying to look better than you really are.*

²Nothing is covered up that won't be discovered; nothing is hidden that won't be exposed. ³Whatever a person says in the dark will be published in the light of day, and whatever a person whispers in private rooms will be broadcast from the housetops.

⁴Listen, My friends, if people are trying to kill you, why be afraid? After you're dead, what more can they do? ⁵⁻⁶Here's whose opinion you should be concerned about: the One who can take your life and then throw you into hell! He's the only One you should fear! *But don't misunderstand: you don't really need to be afraid of God,* because God cares for every little sparrow. How much is a sparrow worth—don't five of them sell for a few cents?* *Since God never loses track of even one little sparrow,* and since you are so much more precious to God than a thousand flocks of sparrows, *and since God knows you in every de-*

12:6 Two small coins

*tail*—down to the number of hairs on your head at this moment—*you can be secure and unafraid of any person, and* you have nothing to fear from God *either.*

⁸*That's why I keep telling you not to be intimidated.* If you identify unashamedly with Me before others, I, the Son of Man, will affirm you before God and all the heavenly messengers. ⁹But if you deny Me before others, you will be denied before God and all the heavenly messengers. ¹⁰People can speak a word against Me, the Son of Man, and the sin is forgivable. *But they can go too far,* slandering the testimony of the Holy Spirit by rejecting His message about Me, and they won't be forgiven for that.

¹¹So you can anticipate that you will be put on trial before the synagogues and religious officials. Don't worry how you'll respond, and don't worry what you should say. ¹²The Holy Spirit will give you the words to say at the moment when you need them.

*I*n the next several episodes, the theme of money is central. Notice how much Jesus has to say about money. He seems to suggest that money in the kingdom of God is valued in a very different way. He then will move from the topic of money to the topic of complacency. Are the two related? Could Jesus be saying that an excessive concern for money can easily turn the spiritual life into a lukewarm, halfhearted affair?

¹³A person in the crowd got Jesus' attention.

**Person in** | Teacher, intervene and tell my brother to share the
**the Crowd** | family inheritance with me.

Jesus | ¹⁴Since when am I your judge or arbitrator?

¹⁵Then He used that opportunity to speak to the crowd.

Jesus | You'd better be on your guard against any type of
greed, for a person's life is not about having a lot of
possessions.
¹⁶(Then, beginning another parable) A wealthy
man owned some land that produced a huge harvest. ¹⁷He often thought to himself, "I have a prob-
lem here. I don't have anywhere to store all my
crops. What should I do? ¹⁸I know! I'll tear down my
small barns and build even bigger ones, and then
I'll have plenty of storage space for my grain and all
my other goods. ¹⁹Then I'll be able to say to myself,
'I have it made! I can relax and take it easy for years!
So I'll just sit back, eat, drink, and have a good
time!' "
²⁰Then God interrupted his conversation with
himself. "Excuse Me, Mr. Brilliant, but your time
has come. Tonight you will die. Now who will enjoy
everything you've earned and saved?"
²¹This is how it will be for people who accumu-
late huge assets for themselves but have no assets

in relation to God. [22](Then, to His disciples) This is why I keep telling you not to worry about anything in life—about what you'll eat, about how you'll clothe your body. [23]Life is more than food, and the body is more than fancy clothes. [24]Think about those crows flying over there: do they plant and harvest crops? Do they own silos or barns? *Look at them fly.* It looks like God is taking pretty good care of them, doesn't it? Remember that you are more precious to God than birds! [25]Which one of you can add a single hour to your life or eighteen inches* to your height by worrying really hard? [26]If worry can't change anything, why do you do it so much?

[27]Think about those beautiful wild lilies growing over there. They don't work up a sweat toiling for needs or wants—they don't worry about clothing. Yet the great King Solomon never had an outfit that was half as glorious as theirs!

[28]Look at the grass growing over there. One day it's thriving in the fields. The next day it's being used as fuel. *If God takes such good care of such transient things,* how much more you can depend on God to care for you, weak in faith as you are. [29]Don't reduce your life to the pursuit of food and drink; don't let your mind be filled with anxiety. [30]People of the world who don't know God pursue these things, *but you have a Father caring for you,* a Father who knows all your needs.

---

**12:25** One cubit

³¹*Since you don't need to worry—about security and safety, about food and clothing—*then pursue God's kingdom *first and foremost*, and these other things will come to you as well.

³²My little flock, don't be afraid. *God is your Father, and* your Father's great joy is to give you His kingdom.

³³That means you can sell your possessions and give generously to the poor. You can have a different kind of savings plan: one that never depreciates, one that never defaults, one that can't be plundered by crooks or destroyed by natural calamities. ³⁴*Your treasure will be stored in the heavens,* and since your treasure is there, your heart will be lodged there as well.

³⁵⁻³⁶*I'm not just talking theory. There is urgency in all this.* If you're apathetic and complacent, then you'll miss the moment of opportunity. You should be wide awake and on your toes like servants who are waiting for their master to return from a big wedding reception. They'll have their shoes on and their lamps lit so they can open the door for him as soon as he arrives home. ³⁷How fortunate those servants will be when the master knocks and they open the door immediately! You know what the master will do? He'll put on an apron, sit them down at the kitchen table, and he'll serve them a midnight snack. ³⁸The later he comes home—whether it's at midnight or even later, just

before dawn—the more fortunate the alert servants will be.

³⁹*In contrast, imagine a complacent, apathetic household manager who has no sense of urgency. He wanders out one night and leaves the door unlocked, and some thieves sneak in and empty the place.* If he had been aware that thieves *were waiting in the bushes* and what hour they were coming, [he would have watched and]* he never would have left the house! ⁴⁰I'm trying to tell you that these are times for alertness, times requiring a sense of urgency and intensity, because *like the master in the first story or the thief in the second,* the Son of Man shows up by surprise.

**Peter** | ⁴¹Lord, I'm not sure if this parable is intended only for us disciples or if this is for everyone else too.

**Jesus** | ⁴²Imagine the stories of two household managers, and decide for yourself which one is faithful and smart. Each household manager is told by his master to *take good care of all his possessions* and to oversee the other employees—*the butlers, cooks, gardeners, and so on.* ⁴³One servant immediately busies himself in doing just what he was told. His master eventually comes to check on him ⁴⁴and rewards him with a major promotion and with more responsibility and trust. ⁴⁵The other household manager thinks, "Look, my boss is going to be gone

---

**12:39** The earliest manuscripts omit the bracketed portion.

for a long time. *I can be complacent; there's no urgency here.* " So he beats the other employees—the women as well as the men. He sits around *like a slob*, eating and getting drunk. ⁴⁶Then the boss comes home unexpectedly and catches him by surprise. One household manager will be fortunate indeed, and the other will be cut into pieces and thrown out.

⁴⁷Now if a servant who is given clear instructions by his master doesn't follow those instructions but instead is complacent and apathetic, then he will be punished severely. ⁴⁸But if a servant doesn't know what his master expects and behaves badly, then he will receive a lighter punishment. If you are given much, much will be required of you. If much is entrusted to you, much will be expected of you.

⁴⁹*This is serious business we're involved in.* My mission is to send a purging fire on the earth! In fact, I can hardly wait to see the smoke rising. ⁵⁰I have a kind of ceremonial washing* to go through, and I can't relax until My mission is accomplished! ⁵¹Do you think I've come with a nice little message of peace? No way. Believe Me, My message will divide. ⁵²It will divide a household of five into three against two or two against three. ⁵³It will divide father against son and son against father; mother against daughter and daughter against mother; mother-in-

---

12:50 Literally, immersion

law against daughter-in-law and daughter-in-law against mother-in-law.

[54](speaking to the crowd) You see a cloud arise *from the sea* in the west, and you can say, "Here comes a shower!" And you're right. [55]Or you feel the hot wind blowing in from *the desert in* the south and you say, "It's going to be really hot!" And you're right. [56]Listen, hypocrites! You can predict the weather by paying attention to the sky and the earth, but why can't you interpret the urgency of this present moment? [57]Why don't you see it for yourselves?

[58]Imagine you're being sued. You and your accuser are on your way to court. Wouldn't you do everything in your power to settle out of court before you stand before the magistrate? After all, he might drag you to stand before the judge, and the judge might hand you over to the police, and they might throw you in jail. [59]Once you're in jail, it's too late: you're not going anywhere until you've paid in full.

## YEAST THAT PUFFS UP

¹As He said this, some people told Him the latest news about a group of Galilean pilgrims *in Jerusalem—a group not unlike Jesus' own entourage.* Pilate butchered them *while they were at worship*, their own blood mingling with the blood of their sacrifices.

**Jesus** | ²Do you think these Galileans *were somehow being singled out for their sins*, that they were worse than any other Galileans, because they suffered this terrible death? ³Of course not. But listen, if you do not consider God's ways and truly change, then friends, you should prepare to face His judgment and eternal death.

⁴*Speaking of current events,* you've all heard about the 18 people killed *in that building accident* when the tower in Siloam fell. Were they extraordinarily bad people, worse than anyone else in Jerusalem, *so that they would deserve such an untimely death*? ⁵Of course not. *But all the buildings of Jerusalem will come crashing down on you* if you don't wake up and change direction now.

⁶(following up with this parable) A man has a fig tree planted in his vineyard. One day he comes out looking for fruit on it, but there are no figs. ⁷He says to the vineyard keeper, "Look at this tree. For three years I've come hoping to find some fresh figs, but

what do I find? Nothing. So just go ahead and cut it down. Why waste the space with a fruitless tree?"

⁸The vineyard keeper replies, "Give it another chance, sir. Give me one more year working with it. I'll cultivate the soil and heap on some manure to fertilize it. ⁹If it surprises us and bears fruit next year, that will be great, but if not, then we'll cut it down."

¹⁰Around this time, He was teaching in a synagogue on the Sabbath, *the Jewish day of rest.* ¹¹A woman there had been sick for 18 years; she was weak, hunched over, and unable to stand up straight. ¹²⁻¹³Jesus placed His hands on her and suddenly she could stand straight again. She started praising God, ¹⁴but the synagogue official was indignant because Jesus had not kept their Sabbath regulations by performing this healing.

**Synagogue Official** | Look, there are six other days when it's appropriate to get work done. Come on those days to be healed, not on the Sabbath!

**Jesus** | ¹⁵You *religious leaders* are such hypocrites! Every single one of you unties his ox or donkey from its manger every single Sabbath Day, and then you lead it out to get a drink of water, right? ¹⁶Do you care more about your farm animals than you care about this woman, one of Abraham's daughters, oppressed by Satan for 18 years? Can't we untie her from her oppression on the Sabbath?

[17]As the impact of His words settled in, His critics were humiliated, but everyone else loved what Jesus said and celebrated everything He was doing.

**Jesus**
*(explaining)*

[18]Do you want to understand the kingdom of God? Do you want Me to tell you what it's like? [19]It's like a single mustard seed that someone took and planted in his garden. That tiny seed grew and became a tree so large that the birds could fly in and make their nests in its branches.

[20]Do you want Me to tell you what the kingdom of God is like? [21]It's like some yeast which a woman hid within a huge quantity of flour; soon the whole batch of dough was rising.

[22]He was pressing toward Jerusalem, His journey taking Him through various towns and villages. In each one, He taught the people. [23]Once a person asked this question:

**Inquiring Individual**

Lord, will only a few people be rescued?

**Jesus**

[24]Strive to enter through the narrow door now, because many people—hear Me on this—will try to enter *later on* and will not be able to. [25]Imagine you want to enter someone's home, but you wait until after the homeowner has shut the door. Then you stand outside and bang on the door, and you say, "Sir, please open the door for us!" But he will answer, "I don't know where you're from."

²⁶Then you'll say, "Just a minute. We ate and drank with you, and you taught in our streets." ²⁷But he'll say, "Sorry, I have no idea where you're from. Leave me, all of you evildoers." ²⁸Then you'll see something that will make you cry and grind your teeth together—you'll see Abraham and Isaac and Jacob and all the prophets in the kingdom of God, but you yourselves will be on the outside looking in.

²⁹And then you'll see people streaming in from east and west, from north and south, gathering around the table in the kingdom of God, *but you'll be on the outside looking in.* ³⁰That's how it will be; some are last now who will be first then, and some are first now who will be last then.

³¹Right then some Pharisees came and warned Him.

Pharisees | You'd better get out of here because Herod is plotting Your murder.

Jesus | ³²You can give that sly fox this message: "Watch as I cast out demons and perform healings today and tomorrow, and on the third day I'll reach My destination. ³³But for today and tomorrow and the next day, I have to continue My journey, for no prophet should perish outside of Jerusalem."

³⁴O Jerusalem! O Jerusalem! You kill the prophets and you stone the messengers who are sent to you. How often I wanted to gather in your

children as a hen gathers in her chicks under her wings, but you were not willing to come to Me. [35]Look now, your house is abandoned and empty. You won't see Me until you welcome Me with the words *of the Psalms*, "Anyone who comes in the name of the Eternal One will be blessed!"*

---

**13:35** Psalm 118:26

## PLACE OF HONOR

¹Another Sabbath Day came and Jesus was invited to an official's home for a meal. This fellow was a leader of the Pharisees, and Jesus was still under close surveillance by them. ²Jesus noticed a man suffering from a swelling disorder. ³He questioned the religious scholars and Pharisees.

> **Jesus** | Is it permitted by traditions and the Hebrew Scriptures to heal people on the Sabbath, or is it forbidden?

⁴They didn't reply. Then Jesus healed the man and sent him on his way.

> **Jesus** | ⁵Would any single one of you leave his son* or even his ox in a well on the Sabbath if he had fallen into it, or would you pull him out immediately?

⁶They still didn't reply.
⁷Then He noticed how the guests were jockeying for places of honor at the dinner, so He gave them advice.

> **Jesus** | ⁸Whenever someone invites you to a wedding dinner, don't sit at the head table. Someone more

---

**14:5** Some manuscripts read "donkey."

important than you might also have been invited, [9]and your host will have to humiliate you publicly by telling you to give your seat to the other guest and to go find an open seat in the back of the room. [10]Instead, go and sit in the back of the room. Then your host may find you and say, "My friend! Why are you sitting back here? Come up to this table near the front!" Then you will be publicly honored in front of everyone. [11]Listen, if you lift yourself up, you'll be put down, but if you humble yourself, you'll be honored.

[12]Jesus still wasn't finished. Now He turned to the host who had invited Him to this gathering.

Jesus | When you host a dinner or banquet, don't invite your friends, your brothers, your relatives, or your rich neighbors. If you do, they might invite you to a party of their own, and you'll be repaid for your kindness. [13]Instead, invite the poor, the amputees, the cripples, the blind. [14]Then you'll be blessed because they can never repay you. Your reward will come from God at the resurrection of the just and good.

Guest | [15]Blessed is everyone who will eat bread in the kingdom of God!

Jesus | [16]A man once hosted a huge banquet and invited

many guests. ¹⁷When the time came, he sent his servant to tell the guests who had agreed to come, "We're ready! Come now!" ¹⁸But then every single guest began to make excuses. One said, *"Oh, I'm sorry.* I just bought some land and I need to go see it. Please excuse me." Another said, *"So sorry.* I just bought five pairs of oxen. I need to go check them out. Please excuse me." Another said, "I just got married, so I can't come."

²¹The servant returned and reported their responses to his master. His master was angry and told the servant, "Go out quickly to the streets and alleys around town and bring the poor, the amputees, the blind, and the cripples."

²²The servant came back again: "Sir, I've done as you said, but there is still more room." ²³And the host said, "Well then, go out to the highways and hedges and bring in the complete strangers you find there, until my house is completely full. ²⁴One thing is for sure, not one single person on the original guest list shall enjoy this banquet."

²⁵Great crowds joined Him on His journey, and He turned to them.

Jesus | ²⁶If any of you come to Me without hating your own father, mother, wife, children, brothers, sisters, and yes, even your own life, you can't be My disciple. ²⁷If you don't carry your own cross *as if to your own execution* as you follow Me, you can't be part of My movement. [28]Just imagine that you want to build a tower. Wouldn't you first sit down and estimate the cost to be sure you have enough to finish what you start? [29]If you lay the foundation but then can't afford to finish the tower, everyone will mock you: [30]"Look at that guy who started something that he couldn't finish!"

[31]Or imagine a king gearing up to go to war. Wouldn't he begin by sitting down *with his advisors* to determine whether his 10,000 troops could defeat the opponent's 20,000 troops? [32]If not, he'll send a peace delegation quickly and negotiate a peace treaty. [33]In the same way, if you want to be My disciple, it will cost you everything. *Don't underestimate that cost!*

[34]Don't be like salt that has lost its taste. How can its saltiness be restored? *Flavorless salt is absolutely worthless.* [35]You can't even use it as fertilizer, so it's worth less than manure! Don't just listen to My words here. Get the deeper meaning.

## THE DELINQUENT SON

¹Jesus became increasingly popular among *notorious* sinners—tax collectors and other social outcasts. ²The Pharisees and religious scholars noticed this.

| | |
|---|---|
| **Pharisees and Religious Scholars** | This man welcomes immoral people and enjoys their company over a meal! |
| **Jesus** *(with another parable)* | ³⁻⁴Wouldn't every single one of you, if you have 100 sheep and lose one, leave the 99 in their grazing lands and go out searching for the lost sheep until you find it? ⁵When you find the lost sheep, wouldn't you hoist it up on your shoulders, feeling wonderful? ⁶And when you go home, wouldn't you call together your friends and neighbors? Wouldn't you say, "Come over and celebrate with me, because I've found my lost sheep"? ⁷This is how it is in heaven. They're happier over one sinner who changes his way of life than they are over 99 good and just people who don't need to change their ways of life.  ⁸Or imagine a woman who has 10 silver coins. She loses one. Doesn't she light a lamp, sweep the whole house, and search diligently until that coin is found? ⁹And when she finds it, doesn't she invite her friends and neighbors and say, "Celebrate with me! I've found that silver coin that I lost"? ¹⁰Can't |

you understand? There is joy in the presence of all God's angels over even one sinner who changes his way of life.

[11]Once there was this man who had two sons. [12]One day the younger son came to his father and said, "Father, eventually I'm going to inherit my share of your estate. Rather than waiting until you die, I want you to give me my share now." And so the father *liquidated assets* and divided them. [13]A few days passed and this younger son gathered all his wealth and set off on a journey to a distant land. Once there he wasted everything he owned on wild living. [14]He was broke, a terrible famine struck that land, and he felt desperately hungry and in need. [15]He got a job with one of the locals, who sent him into the fields to feed the pigs. [16]The young man felt so miserably hungry that he wished he could eat the slop the pigs were eating. Nobody gave him anything.

[17]So he had this moment of self-reflection: "*What am I doing here?* Back home, my father's hired servants have plenty of food. Why am I here starving to death? [18]I'll get up and return to my father, and I'll say, "Father, I have done wrong—wrong against God and against you. [19]I have forfeited any right to be treated like your son, but I'm wondering if you'd treat me as one of your hired servants?" [20]So he got up and returned to his father. The father looked off in the distance and saw the young man

returning. He felt compassion for his son and ran out to him, enfolded him in an embrace, and kissed him.

²¹The son said, "Father, I have done a terrible wrong in God's sight and in your sight too. I have forfeited any right to be treated as your son."

²²But the father turned to his servants and said, "Quick! Bring the best robe we have and put it on him. Put a ring on his finger and shoes on his feet. ²³Go get the fattest calf and butcher it. Let's have a feast and celebrate ²⁴because my son was dead and is alive again. He was lost and has been found." So they had this huge party.

²⁵Now the man's older son was still out in the fields working. He came home at the end of the day and heard music and dancing. ²⁶He called one of the servants and asked what was going on. ²⁷The servant said, "Your brother has returned, and your father has butchered the fattest calf to celebrate his safe return."

²⁸The older brother got really angry and refused to come inside, so his father came out and pleaded with him to join the celebration. ²⁹But he argued back, "Listen, all these years I've worked hard for you. I've never disobeyed one of your orders. But how many times have you even given me a little goat to roast for a party with my friends? Not once! *This is not fair!* ³⁰So this son of yours comes, this wasteful delinquent who has spent your hard-

earned wealth on loose women, and what do you do? You butcher the fattest calf from our herd!"

³¹The father replied, "My son, you are always with me, and all I have is yours. ³²Isn't it right to join in the celebration and be happy? This is your brother we're talking about. He was dead and is alive again; he was lost and is found again!"

*T*he parable ends. Jesus never tells us how it comes out. Did the older brother join the party and reconcile with his younger, wayward brother? Or did he stay outside, fuming over the seeming injustice of his father's extravagant love? The story remains unresolved because it is, in fact, an invitation—an invitation to the Pharisees and other opponents of Jesus to join Him in welcoming sinners and other outsiders into the joyful party of the Kingdom.

## WHO WILL YOU SERVE?

¹Here's a parable He told the disciples:

**Jesus** | Once there was a rich *and powerful* man who had an asset manager. One day, the man received word that his asset manager was squandering his assets.

²The rich man brought in the asset manager and said, "You've been accused of wrongdoing. I want a full and accurate accounting of all your financial transactions because you are really close to being fired."

³The manager said to himself, "*Oh, no!* Now what am I going to do? I'm going to lose my job here, and I'm too weak to dig ditches and too proud to beg. ⁴I have an idea. This plan will mean that I have a lot of hospitable friends when I get fired."

⁵So the asset manager set up appointments with each person who owed his master money. He said to the first debtor, "How much do you owe my boss?" ⁶The debtor replied, "A hundred barrels of oil."* The manager said, "I'm discounting your bill by half. Just write 50 on this contract." ⁷Then he said to the second debtor, "How much do you owe?" This fellow said, "A hundred bales of wheat."* The manager

---

**16:6** About 600-800 gallons
**16:7** About 700 bushels

said, "I'm discounting your debt by 20 percent. Just write down 80 bales on this contract."

[8]When the manager's boss realized what he had done, he congratulated him for at least being clever. That's how it is: those attuned to this evil age are more clever in dealing with their affairs than the enlightened are in dealing with their affairs!

[9]*Learn some lessons from this crooked but clever asset manager.* Realize that the purpose of money is to strengthen friendships, to provide opportunities for being generous and kind. Eventually money will be useless to you—but if you use it generously to serve others, you will be welcomed joyfully into your eternal destination.

[10]If you're faithful in small-scale matters, you'll be faithful with far bigger responsibilities. If you're crooked in small responsibilities, you'll be no different in bigger things. [11]If you can't even handle a small thing like money, who's going to entrust you with spiritual riches that really matter? [12]If you don't manage well someone else's assets that are entrusted to you, who's going to give over to you important spiritual and personal relationships to manage?

[13]Imagine you're a servant and you have two masters giving you orders. *One tells you to do one thing, and the other tells you to do the opposite. What are you going to do?* You can't serve both, so you'll either hate the first and love the second, or you'll faith-

fully serve the first and despise the second. One master is God and the other is money. You can't serve them both.

[14]The Pharisees overheard all this, and they started mocking Jesus because they really loved money.

**Jesus**
*(to the Pharisees)*

[15]*You've made your choice.* Your ambition is to look good in front of other people, not God. But God sees through to your hearts. He values things differently from you. The goals you and your peers are reaching for God detests.

[16]The law and the prophets had their role until the coming of John *the Preacher.* Since John's arrival, the good news of the kingdom of God has been taught while people are clamoring to enter it. [17]*That's not to say that God's rules for living are useless.* The stars in the sky and the earth beneath your feet will pass away before one letter of God's rules for living become worthless.

[18]*Take God's rules regarding marriage for example.* If a man divorces his wife and marries somebody else, then it's still adultery *because that man has broken his vow to God.* And if a man marries a woman divorced from her husband, he's committing adultery *for the same reason.*

[19]There was this rich man who had everything—purple clothing of fine quality and high fashion, gourmet meals every day, and a large house. [20]Just

outside his front gate lay this poor *homeless* fellow named Lazarus. Lazarus was covered in ugly skin lesions. [21]He was so hungry he wished he could scavenge scraps from the rich man's trash. Dogs would come and lick the sores on his skin. [22]The poor fellow died and was carried on the arms of the heavenly messengers to the embrace of Abraham. Then the rich fellow died and was buried [23]and found himself in the place of the dead. In his torment, he looked up and off in the distance he saw Abraham, with Lazarus in his embrace.

[24]He shouted out, "Father Abraham! Please show me mercy! Would you send *that beggar* Lazarus to dip his fingertip in water and cool my tongue? These flames are hot, and I'm in agony!"

[25]But Abraham said, "Son, you seem to be forgetting something: your life was full to overflowing with comforts and pleasures, and the life of Lazarus was just as full with suffering and pain. So now is his time of comfort, and now is your time of agony. [26]Besides, a great canyon separates you and us. Nobody can cross over from our side to yours, or from your side to ours."

[27]"Please, Father *Abraham,* I beg you," the formerly rich man continued, "send Lazarus to my father's house. [28]I have five brothers there, *and they're on the same path I was on.* If Lazarus warns them, they'll choose another path and won't end up here in torment."

²⁹But Abraham said, *"Why send Lazarus?* They already have the law of Moses and the writings of the prophets to instruct them. Let your brothers hear them."

³⁰"No, Father Abraham," he said, *"they're already ignoring the law and the prophets.* But if someone came back from the dead, then they'd listen for sure; then they'd change their way of life."

³¹Abraham answered, "If they're not listening to Moses and the prophets, they won't be convinced even if someone comes back from the dead."

*Y*ou've noticed, no doubt, how the theme of money and wealth has come up again and again. It's what really motivates the Pharisees, it turns out. We might say that money is God's top competitor. In the previous parable, Jesus really turns the tables. The rich man, who represents what most people wish they could become, turns out to be the one who is hopeless in God's judgment; he was rich in possessions but poor in compassion, and compassion is what God was measuring, not wealth. The kingdom of God, Jesus is making clear, calls rich people to stop working to increase their personal wealth portfolio; instead, it challenges them to join God by using their wealth and power on behalf of the poor. That same theme will come up several times in later episodes of Luke's story.

# *Luke 17*

## ONLY ONE RETURNED

**Jesus**
*(to His disciples)*

¹You can't stop temptations to do wrong from coming. But how tragic it will be for the person who becomes the source of the temptation! ²It would be better if a millstone were hung around his neck and he were thrown into the sea, than that he should offend one of these little ones.

³So each of you needs to be careful. *Instead of encouraging wrongdoing in any way, be a person who overcomes wrongdoing.* If your brother sins [against you],* confront him about it, and if he has a change of mind and heart, then forgive him. ⁴Even if he wrongs you seven times in a single day, if he turns back to you each time and says he's sorry and will change, you must forgive him.

**Emissaries**

⁵*We don't have enough faith for this!* Help our faith to grow!

**Jesus**
*(pointing to a nearby mulberry tree)*

⁶*It's not like you need a huge amount of faith.* If you just had faith the size of a single, tiny mustard seed, you could say to this huge tree, "Pull up your roots and replant yourself in the sea," and it would *fly through the sky and* do what you said. *So even a little faith can accomplish the seemingly impossible.*

---

**17:3** The earliest manuscripts omit this portion.

*⁷Imagine this scenario.* You have a servant—say he's been out plowing a field or taking care of the sheep—and he comes in hot and sweaty from his work. Are you going to say, *"You poor thing!* Come in and sit down right away"? Of course not! ⁸Wouldn't you be more likely to say, "First, cook my supper and set the table, and then after I've eaten, you can get something to eat and drink for yourself"? ⁹And after your servant has done everything you told him to do, are you going to make a big deal about it and thank him? [I don't think so!]* ¹⁰Now apply this situation to yourselves. When you've done everything I'm telling you to do, just say, "We're servants, unworthy of extra consideration or thanks; we're just doing our duty."

¹¹Jesus was still pressing toward Jerusalem, taking a road that went along the border between Samaria *(considered undesirable territory)* and Galilee. ¹²On the outskirts of a border town along this road, He was greeted from a distance by a group of 10 people who were under quarantine because of an ugly and disgusting skin disease known as leprosy.

**Lepers** | ¹³Jesus, Master, show mercy to us!
*(shouting across the distance)* |

**Jesus** | ¹⁴Go now and present yourselves to the priests *for inspection of your disease.*

They went, and before they reached the priests, their skin disease was healed, *leaving no trace of the disease that scarred them and separated them from the community.*

---

17:9 The earliest manuscripts omit this portion.

¹⁵One of them, the instant he realized he had been healed, turned and ran back to Jesus, shouting praises to God. ¹⁶He prostrated himself facedown at Jesus' feet.

**Leper** | Thank You! Thank You!

Now this fellow happened to be, *not a Jew,* but a Samaritan.

**Jesus** | ¹⁷Didn't all 10 receive the same healing this fellow did? Where are the other 9? ¹⁸Was the only 1 who came back to give God praise an outsider? ¹⁹(to the Samaritan man) Get up, and go your way. Your faith has made you healthy again.

²⁰Some Pharisees asked Jesus when the kingdom of God would come.

**Jesus** | The kingdom of God comes—but not with signs that you can observe. ²¹People are not going to say, "Look! Here it is!" They're not going to say, "Look! It's over there!" You want to see the kingdom of God? The kingdom of God is already here among you.

²²(to His disciples) Days are coming when you will wish you could see just one of the days of the Son of Man, but you won't see it. ²³People will say, "Look, it's there!" or "Look! It's here!" Don't even bother looking. Don't follow their lead. ²⁴You know how lightning flashes across the sky, bringing light

from one horizon to the other. That's how the Son of Man will be when His time comes.

²⁵But first, He must face many sufferings. He must be rejected by this generation. ²⁶The days of the Son of Man will be like the days of Noah. ²⁷People were eating, drinking, marrying, and being given in marriage. *Everything seemed completely normal* until the day Noah entered the ark. Then it started raining, and soon they were all destroyed by the flood.

²⁸It was just the same in the days of Lot. People were eating, drinking, buying, selling, planting, building, *and carrying on business as usual.* ²⁹But then came the day when Lot left Sodom—a different kind of rain began to fall, and they were all destroyed by fire and sulfur falling from the sky.* ³⁰That's how it will be on the day when the Son of Man is revealed.

³¹When that day comes, if you're on the housetop, don't run inside to try to save any of your belongings. If you're in the field, don't bother running back *to the house.* ³²Remember Lot's wife. *Turning back is fatal for those who do so.* ³³If you try to hold on to your life, it will slip through your fingers; if you let go of your life, you'll keep it. ³⁴Listen, on the day of the Son of Man, two people will be asleep in bed; destruction will take one and the other will be left to survive. ³⁵Two women will

be grinding grain together; destruction will take one and the other will survive. [³⁶Two men will be working out in the field; destruction will overtake one and the other will survive.]*

**Disciples** | ³⁷Where, Lord?

**Jesus** | Where vultures circle over rotting corpses.

17:36 Most manuscripts omit verse 36.

## NO ONE IS GOOD

*T*he theme of prayer has come up again and again. In the next few episodes, Jesus emphasizes the importance of persistence and humility in prayer. Why is prayer so important for Jesus? It's clear that the kingdom of God will not come through valiant efforts or foolproof strategies. It will come as people pray, "may Your kingdom come," with persistence and with humility.

¹He told them a parable, urging them to keep praying and never grow discouraged. The parable went like this:

**Jesus** | ²There was a judge living in a certain city. He showed no respect for God or humanity. ³In that same city there was a widow. Again and again she kept coming to him seeking justice: "Clear my name from my adversary's false accusations!" ⁴He paid no attention to her request for a while, but then he said to himself, "I don't care about what God thinks of me, much less what any mere human thinks. ⁵But this widow is driving me crazy. She's never going to quit coming to see me unless I hear her case and provide her legal protection."

⁶Did you catch what this self-assured judge said? ⁷*If he can be moved to act justly,* won't God bring

justice for His chosen people when they cry to Him day and night? Will He be slow to bring them justice? [8]Mark My words: God will intervene fast with vindication. But here's the question: when the Son of Man comes, will He find anyone who still has faith?

[9]He told another parable—this one addressed to people who were confident in their self-righteousness and looked down on other people with disgust.

Jesus | [10]Imagine two men *walking up a road*, going to the temple to pray. One of them is a Pharisee and the other is a *despised* tax collector. [11]Once inside the temple, the Pharisee stands up and prays this prayer in honor of himself: "God, how I thank You that I am not on the same level as other people—crooks, cheaters, the sexually immoral—like this tax collector over here. [12]*Just look at me!* I fast not once but twice a week, and I faithfully pay my tithes on every penny of income." [13]Over in the corner, the tax collector begins to pray, but he won't even lift his eyes to heaven. He pounds on his chest *in sorrow* and says, "God, be merciful to me, a sinner!"

[14]*Now imagine these two men walking back down the road to their homes.* Listen, it's the tax collector who walks home clean before God, and not the Pharisee, because whoever lifts himself up will be put down and whoever takes a humble place will be lifted up.

[15]Some people brought infants to Jesus, hoping He would touch them *in blessing*. The disciples rebuked them for doing so, [16]but Jesus called to the people.

Jesus | Let the little children come to Me. Never hinder them! Don't you realize—the kingdom of God belongs to those who are like children? [17]You can depend on this: if you don't receive the Kingdom as a child would, you won't enter it at all.

Public Official | [18]Good Teacher, what do I need to do to inherit the life of the age to come?

Jesus | [19]Why did you just call Me good? No one is good but God—only God. [20]You know what the *Hebrew* Scriptures command: "Do not commit adultery, do not murder, do not steal, do not bear false witness, honor your father and mother."*

Public Official | [21]I've already been doing these things—since I came of age.

Jesus | [22]One thing you still lack—one thing; sell all your possessions and distribute the proceeds to the poor. Then you will have treasure in heaven. Then you can come and follow Me.

---

**18:20** Exodus 20:12-16; Deuteronomy 5:16-20

²³The man heard these words and sadness came over his face, for his wealth was considerable.

Jesus | ²⁴What a hard thing it is for those with much wealth to enter the kingdom of God! ²⁵In fact, it would be easier for a camel to squeeze through the eye of a needle than it would be for a rich person to enter the kingdom of God!

Listeners | ²⁶Then who can be liberated?

Jesus | ²⁷Remember, what is humanly impossible is possible with God.

Peter | ²⁸We have left our homes and followed You.

Jesus | ²⁹I'm telling you the truth: there is nobody who leaves his house or wife or siblings or parents or children for the sake of the kingdom of God ³⁰who will not receive more than he has given up—much more—in this age and in the age to come. He will receive eternal life.

³¹He took the twelve aside and spoke privately to them.

Jesus | Look, *my friends,* we are going up to Jerusalem. Everything the prophets have written about the Son of Man will be fulfilled. ³²He will be handed over to the outsiders. They will mock Him, disgrace

Him, and spit on Him; ³³they will scourge Him, and they will kill Him. And on the third day, He will rise from death.

³⁴But they had no comprehension of what He was talking about. The meaning was hidden from them, and they couldn't grasp it.

³⁵*Picture this:*

Jesus is nearing the city of Jericho. A blind man is sitting there, begging by the roadside. ³⁶He can hear the sounds of the crowd *accompanying Jesus*, and he asks what's going on.

**Crowd** | ³⁷Jesus of Nazareth is passing this way.

³⁸Then the man starts shouting.

**Blind Man** | Jesus, Son of *King* David, show mercy to me!

³⁹The people in the front of the crowd reprimand him and tell him to be quiet, but he just shouts louder.

**Blind Man** | Son of *King* David, show mercy to me!

⁴⁰Jesus stops and tells the people to bring the man over to Him. The man stands in front of Jesus.

**Jesus** | ⁴¹What do you want Me to do for you?

**Blind Man** | Lord, let me receive my sight.

**Jesus** | [42]Receive your sight; your faith has made you well.

[43]At that very instant, the man is able to see. He begins following Jesus, shouting praises to God, and everyone in the crowd, when they see what has happened, starts praising God too.

## INVESTING IN THE KINGDOM

¹Jesus enters Jericho and seems only to be passing through. ²Living in Jericho is a man named Zaccheus. He's the head tax collector and is very rich. ³He is also very short. He wants to see Jesus as He passes through the center of town, but he can't get a glimpse because the crowd blocks his view. ⁴So he runs ahead of the crowd and climbs up into a sycamore tree so he can see Jesus when He passes beneath him.

⁵Jesus comes along and looks up into the tree [, and there He sees Zaccheus].*

> **Jesus** | Zaccheus, hurry down from that tree because I need to stay at your house *tonight*.

⁶Zaccheus scrambles down and joyfully brings Jesus back to his house. ⁷Now the crowd sees this, and they're upset.

> **Crowd** | Jesus has become the houseguest of this fel-
> *(grumbling)* | low who is a notorious sinner.

> **Zaccheus** | ⁸Lord, I am giving half of my goods to the poor, and whomever I have cheated I will pay back four times what I took.

---

19:5 The earliest manuscripts omit this portion.

**Jesus** | ⁹Today, liberation has come to this house, since even Zaccheus is living as a son of Abraham. ¹⁰For the Son of Man came to seek and to liberate the lost.

¹¹The crowd has been listening to all this, and everyone assumes that the kingdom of God is going to appear at any moment, since He's nearing Jerusalem. So He tells them this parable:

**Jesus** | ¹²A ruler once planned a journey to a distant country planning to take the throne of that country and then return home. ¹³Before his departure, he called 10 of his servants and gave them each about 3 months of wages.* "Use this money to buy and sell until I return." ¹⁴After he departed, the people under his rule despised him and sent messengers with a clear message: "We do not want this man to rule over us."

¹⁵He successfully assumed kingship *of the distant country* and returned home. He called his 10 servants together and told them to give an account of their success in doing business with the money he had entrusted to them.

¹⁶The first came before him and said, "Lord, I have made 10 times the amount you

---

**19:13** Greek *mina*

entrusted to me." [17]The ruler replied, "Well done! You're a good servant indeed! Since you have been faithful in handling a small amount of money, I'll entrust you with authority over 10 cities *in my new kingdom.*"

[18]The second came and said, "Lord, I've made five times the original amount." [19]The ruler replied, "I'll entrust you with authority over five cities."

[20]A third came and said, "Lord, I have successfully preserved the money you gave me. I wrapped it up in a napkin and hid it away [21]because I was afraid of you. After all, you're a tough man. You have a way of taking a profit without making an investment and harvesting when you didn't plant any seed."

[22]The ruler replied, "I will condemn you using your very own words, you worthless servant! So I'm a severe man, am I? So I take a profit without making an investment and harvest without planting seed? [23]Then why didn't you invest my money in the bank so I could have at least gained some interest on it?" [24]The ruler told the onlookers, "Take the money I gave him and give it to the one who multiplied my investment by 10."

[25]Then the onlookers replied, "Lord, he already has 10 times the original amount!"

²⁶The ruler responded, "Listen, whoever has some will be given more, and whoever doesn't have anything will lose what he thinks he has. ²⁷And these enemies of mine who didn't want me to rule over them—bring them here and execute them in my presence."

*I*n Jesus' day, as today, many people want to speculate about when the kingdom of God will fully arrive. But Jesus, through the previous parable, makes it clear that such speculation is a waste of time. Instead, people should be busy investing their lives in the kingdom of God. And Luke has made clear what that means in some earlier episodes. In His encounter with the rich young ruler, Jesus invited the man to stop collaborating with the Roman Empire for his own benefit and to switch sides—so he could start working with the kingdom of God for the sake of the poor. The man refused; but soon after, a man named Zaccheus volunteered to do that very thing: to stop working for his own wealth by collaborating with Caesar's kingdom and to start working for justice for the poor by collaborating with God's kingdom. Speculation about the dates and times of the coming of the Kingdom can make us miss the point—we should live, starting now, in the way of the Kingdom.

²⁸When He finished the parable, He pushed onward, climbing the steep hills toward Jerusalem.

²⁹He approached the towns of Bethphage and Bethany, which are near Mount Olivet. He sent two of the disciples ahead.

**Jesus** | [30]Go to the next village. When you enter, you will find a colt tied—a colt that has never been ridden before. Untie it and bring it here. [31]If anyone asks you why you're untying it, just say, "The Lord needs it."

[32]So the two disciples found things just as He had told them. [33]When its owners did indeed ask why they were untying the colt, [34]the disciples answered *as they had been instructed.*

**Disciples** | The Lord needs it.

[35]They brought the colt to Jesus, threw their coats on the colt's back, and then sat Jesus on it. [36]As Jesus rode along, some people began to spread their garments on the road *as a carpet.* [37]When they passed the crest of Mount Olivet and began descending toward Jerusalem, a huge crowd of disciples began to celebrate and praise God with loud shouts, glorifying God for the mighty works they had witnessed.

**Crowd of Disciples** | [38]The King who comes in the name of the Eternal One is blessed!*
Peace in heaven! Glory in the highest!

**Pharisees** (who were in the crowd) | [39]Teacher, tell these people to stop making these wild claims and acting this way!

---

**19:38** Psalm 118:26

Jesus | ⁴⁰Listen—if they were silent, the very rocks would start to shout!

⁴¹When Jerusalem came into view, He looked intently at the city and began to weep.

Jesus | ⁴²How I wish you knew today what would bring peace! But you can't see. ⁴³Days will come when your enemies will build up a siege ramp, and you will be surrounded and contained on every side.* ⁴⁴Your enemies will smash you into rubble and not leave one stone standing on another, and they will cut your children down too, because you did not recognize the day when God's Anointed One visited you.

*I*n this powerful scene as Jesus comes into city, echoing the words of Zechariah 9:9, Jesus shows how His kingdom is upside down compared to the kingdoms of this world. Caesar would enter a town riding a white stallion, accompanied by dignitaries and soldiers with weapons. Jesus comes on a little donkey, cheered by common people waving branches and coats. The contrast between the two ways, He suggests through tears, is the difference between peace and violent destruction.

⁴⁵He entered *Jerusalem* and went into the temple. He began driving out the temple merchants.

---

**19:43** Ezekiel 4:2; 26:8

**Jesus** | ⁴⁶The *Hebrew* Scriptures say, "My house shall be a house of prayer,"* but you have turned it into a shelter for thieves.*

⁴⁷He came back day after day to teach in the temple. The chief priests, the religious scholars, and the leading men of the city wanted to kill Him, ⁴⁸but because He was so popular among the people—who hung upon each word He spoke—they were unable to do anything.

---

19:46 Isaiah 56:7
19:46 Jeremiah 7:11

# Luke 20

## BEWARE OF RELIGIOUS SCHOLARS

¹One day when He was teaching the people in the temple and proclaiming the good news, the chief priests, religious scholars, and elders came up and questioned Him.

**Elders** | ²Tell us by what authority You march into the temple and disrupt our worship. Who gave You this authority?

**Jesus** | ³Let Me ask you a question first. Tell Me this: ⁴was the ritual washing* of John *the Preacher* from God, or was it merely a human thing?

**Chief Priest, Religious Scholars, and Elders**
*(conferring together)* | ⁵If we say it was from God, then He'll ask us why we didn't believe John. ⁶If we say it was merely human, all the people will stone us because they are convinced that John was a true prophet.

⁷So they said they didn't know where John's ritual washing came from.

**Jesus** | ⁸Well then, if you won't answer My question, I won't tell you by what authority I have acted.

⁹He told the people another parable:

---

**20:3** Literally, immersion, an act of repentance

**Jesus** | A man planted a vineyard. He rented it to tenants and went for a long trip to another country. ⁱ⁰At the harvesttime, he sent a servant to the tenants so he could be paid his share of the vineyard's fruit, but the tenants beat the servant and sent him away empty-handed. ¹¹The man sent another servant, and they beat him and treated him disgracefully and sent him away empty-handed too. ¹²He sent a third servant who was injured and thrown out. ¹³Then the vineyard owner said, "Now what am I going to do? I'll send my much-loved son. They should treat him with respect."

¹⁴But when the tenants recognized the owner's son, they said, *"Here's our chance to actually own this vineyard!* Let's kill the owner's heir so we can claim this place as our own!" ¹⁵So they threw him out of the vineyard and murdered him. What do you think the owner will do to these scoundrels?

¹⁶*I'll tell you what he'll do;* he'll come and wipe those tenants out, and he'll give the vineyard to others.

**Crowd** | No! God forbid that this should happen!

**Jesus** | ¹⁷Why then do the *Hebrew* Scriptures contain these words:

> "The stone that the builders rejected
>     has become the very stone
>         that holds up the entire foundation"?*

---

**20:17** Psalm 118:22

¹⁸Everyone who falls on that stone will be broken to fragments, and if that stone falls on anyone, he will be ground to dust.

¹⁹*That was the last straw for* the religious scholars and the chief priests; they were ready to attack Him right then and there. But they couldn't for fear of public opinion, and they realized that Jesus, through this parable, had exposed their violent intentions.

²⁰*Since they couldn't use overt violence against Him, they developed a covert plan.* They would keep Him under constant surveillance. They would send spies, pretending to ask sincere questions, listening for something they could seize upon that would justify His arrest and condemnation under the governor's authority.

**Chief Priest, Religious Scholars, and Elders** | ²¹Teacher, we respect You because You speak and teach only what is right, You show no partiality to anyone, and You truly teach the way of God. ²²So— is it lawful for us to pay taxes to Caesar's *occupying regime*, or should we refuse?

²³He saw through their transparent trick.

**Jesus** | [Why are you trying to trick Me?]* ²⁴Show Me a coin. Whose image and name are on this coin?

**Chief Priest, Religious Scholars, and Elders** | Caesar's.

---

**20:23** The earliest manuscripts omit the end of verse 23.

**Jesus** | $^{25}$Well then, you should give to Caesar whatever is Caesar's, and you should give to God whatever is God's.

$^{26}$Once again they failed to humiliate Him in public or catch Him in a punishable offense. They were confounded by His reply and couldn't say anything in response.

$^{27}$Another group came to test Him—this time from the Sadducees, a *rival party of the Pharisees*, who believe that there is no resurrection.

*I*n addition to the Pharisees, there was a religious sect in Jesus' day called the Sadducees. They were religious conservatives holding to an ancient tradition in Judaism that didn't believe in an afterlife. Their disbelief in an afterlife seemed to make them conclude, "There's only one life, and this is it, so you'd better play it safe." That meant that they were very happy to collaborate with the Romans—and make a healthy profit—rather than risk any kind of rebellion or revolt. For this reason, they were closely allied with another group called the Herodians, allies of Caesar's puppet king Herod. Their contemporaries, the Pharisees, who believed in an afterlife, were more prone to risk their lives in a rebellion since they believed martyrs would be rewarded with resurrection. For this reason, the Pharisees were closely allied with the Zealots, who were more overtly revolutionary. But the Pharisees too were very fond of money. It's interesting to see each group try to trap Jesus and then to watch Jesus turn the tables on them, using each encounter to shed more light on the message of the kingdom of God. In case after

> case, as we've seen already and as you'll see again shortly, Jesus
> brings His hearers to the heart of the matter; and again and again,
> the bottom-line issue is money.

**Sadducees** | [28]Teacher, Moses wrote *in the Hebrew Scriptures* that a man must marry his brother's wife and the new couple should bear children for his brother if his brother dies without heirs.* [29]Well, once there were seven brothers, and the first took a wife and then died without fathering children. [30]The second [took her as his wife and then he died childless,]* [31]and then the third, and so on through the seven. They all died leaving no children. [32]Finally, the woman died too. [33]*Here's our question:* in the resurrection, whose wife will she be, since all seven had her for a while? *Will she be the wife of seven men at once?*

**Jesus** | [34]The children of this era marry and are given in marriage, [35]but those who are considered worthy to attain the resurrection of the dead in the coming era do not marry and are not given in marriage. [36]They are beyond mortality; they are on the level of heavenly messengers; they are children of God and children of the resurrection. [37]*Since you brought up the issue of resurrection,* even Moses made clear in the passage about the burning bush that the dead are,

20:28 Deuteronomy 25:5
20:30 The earliest manuscripts omit the end of verse 30.

in fact, raised. After all, he calls the Lord the God of Abraham, Isaac, and Jacob.* [38]*By Moses' time, they were all dead,* but God isn't God of the dead, but of the living. So all live to God.

**Religious Scholars** | [39]Teacher, that was a good answer.

[40]After this, no one had the courage to ask Him any more questions. [41]But He asked them a question.

**Jesus** | How is it that people say the Liberating King is David's descendant? [42]Don't you remember how David himself wrote in the Psalms,

> "The Eternal One said to my Lord, *the King*:
>    'Sit here at My right hand,
>       *in the place of honor and power.*
> [43]And I will gather Your enemies together,
>       *lead them in on hands and knees,*
>    and You will rest Your feet on their
>       backs."*

Did you hear that? David calls his son "Lord." Elders don't respect their younger that way. How is David's son also "Lord"?

[45]Jesus turns to His disciples, speaking loud enough for the others to hear.

---

**20:37** Exodus 3:6,15
**20:42-43** Psalm 110:1

Jesus | ⁴⁶Beware of the religious scholars. They like to parade around in long robes. They love being greeted in the marketplaces. They love taking the best seats in the synagogues. They adore being seated around the head table at banquets. ⁴⁷But *in their greed* they rob widows of their houses and *cover up their greed* with long pretentious prayers. Their condemnation will be all the worse *because of their hypocrisy.*

BLOOD COVENANT

¹And then He turned His attention from the religious scholars to some wealthy people who were depositing their donations in the offering boxes. ²A widow, obviously poor, came up and dropped two copper coins in one of the boxes.

Jesus | ³I'm telling you the truth, this poor widow has made a bigger contribution than all of those rich fellows. ⁴They're just giving from their surplus, but she is giving from her poverty—she's giving all she has to give.

⁵Some people were impressed with the temple's opulence—the precious stones and expensive decorations—but Jesus countered their observations.

Jesus | ⁶Go ahead, look around, and be impressed, but days are coming when one stone will not be left standing on another. Everything here will be demolished.

Crowd | ⁷When will this happen, Teacher? What signs will tell us this is about to occur?

Jesus | ⁸Be careful. It's easy to be deceived. Many people will come claiming to have My authority. They'll shout, "I'm the One!" or "The time is now!" Don't take a step in their direction. [9]You'll hear about wars and conflicts, but don't be frightened at all because these things must surely come, although they don't signify the immediate coming of the end.

[10]*You can count on this:* nation will attack nation, and kingdom will make war on kingdom. [11]There will be disturbances around the world—from great earthquakes to famines to epidemics. Terrifying things will happen, and there will be shocking signs from heaven. [12]But before any of this happens, they will capture you and persecute you. They'll send you to synagogues *for trial* and to prisons *for punishment*; you'll stand before kings and government officials for the sake of My name. [13]This will be your opportunity—your opportunity to tell your story. [14]Make up your mind in advance not to plan your strategy for answering their questions, [15]for when the time comes, I will give you the words to say—wise words—which none of your adversaries will be able to answer or argue against. [16]Your own parents, brothers, relatives, and friends will turn on you and turn you in. Some of you will be killed, [17]and all of you will be hated by everyone for the sake of My name.

[18]But whatever happens, not a single hair of your heads will be harmed. [19]By enduring all of these things, you will find *not loss but gain*—not death but authentic life.

[20]Here's how you will know that the destruction

of Jerusalem *and her temple* is imminent: Jerusalem will be surrounded by armies. [21]When that happens, *there's only one thing to do:* if you're in Judea, flee to the mountains, and if you're inside the city, escape, and if you're outside the city, stay there—don't enter— [22]because the time has come for the promised judgment to fall. [23]How sad it will be for all the pregnant women, for all the nursing mothers in those days! All the land of Israel and all her people will feel the distress, the anger, falling on them *like rain.* [24]The sword will cut some down, and the outsider nations will take others captive, and this holy city, this Jerusalem, will be trampled upon by the outsiders until their times are fulfilled.

[25]*There will be earth-shattering events*—the heavens themselves will seem to be shaken with signs in the sun, in the moon, and in the stars. And across the earth the *outsider* nations will feel powerless and terrified in the face of a roaring flood *of fear and foreboding*, crashing like tidal waves upon them. [26]"What's happening to the world?" people will wonder. The cosmic order will be destabilized. [27]And then, at that point, they will see the Son of Man coming in a cloud with power and blazing glory. [28]So when the troubles begin, *don't be afraid.* Look up, raise your head high, because the truth is that your liberation is fast approaching.

[29](continuing with a parable) Look over there at that fig tree—and all the trees surrounding it.

³⁰When the leaves break out of their buds, nobody has to tell you that summer is approaching; it's obvious to you. ³¹*It's the same in the larger scheme of things.* When you see all these things happening, you can be confident that the kingdom of God is approaching. ³²I'm telling you the truth: this generation will not pass from the scene before everything I'm telling you has occurred. ³³Heaven and earth will cease to exist before My words ever fail.

³⁴So be careful. Guard your hearts. They can be made heavy with moral laxity, with drunkenness, with the hassles of daily life. Then the day I've been telling you about might catch you unaware and trap you. ³⁵Because it's coming—nobody on earth will escape it. ³⁶So you have to stay alert, praying that you'll be able to escape the coming trials so you can stand tall in the presence of the Son of Man.

³⁷⁻³⁸Through this whole period of time, He taught in the temple each day. People would arrive at the temple early in the morning to listen. Then, at day's end, He would leave the city and sleep on Mount Olivet.

## I Sent You with Not Even Sandals

*J*esus taught of a judgment to come and the destruction of the temple. The crowds were intrigued with His teaching, but the religious leaders were increasingly nervous. All things moved toward a collision of ideas and faith at the most important feast of the year.

¹*This daily pattern continued* as they came closer to the holiday of Unleavened Bread, also known as the Passover. ²The chief priests and religious scholars continued looking for a way to kill Jesus; they hadn't been able to act yet due to their fear of the people's reaction. ³At this point, Satan entered into one of the twelve, Judas (also called Iscariot). ⁴Judas set up a private meeting with the chief priests and the captains of the temple police to discuss a plan for betraying Jesus and putting Him in their hands. ⁵*This was just the kind of break they had been waiting for,* so they were thrilled and agreed to a handsome payment. ⁶Everything was settled, and Judas simply waited for the right moment, when the crowds weren't around, to betray Jesus into their custody.

⁷They came to the Day of Unleavened Bread, a holy day when a special lamb (called the Passover lamb) had to be sacrificed. ⁸Jesus chose Peter and John and gave them instructions.

**Jesus** | Go and make all the necessary preparations for the Passover meal so we can eat together.

Peter | ⁹Where do You want us to make preparations?
and John |

Jesus | ¹⁰When you enter the city, you'll encounter a man
carrying a jar of water. Just follow him *wherever he
goes*, and when he enters a house, ¹¹tell the homeowner, "The Teacher has this question for you:
'Where is the guest room where I can share the
Passover meal with My disciples?'" ¹²He'll show you
a spacious second-story room that has all the necessary furniture. That's where you should prepare our
meal.

¹³They did as He said and found everything just as He said it would
be, and they prepared the Passover meal.

¹⁴When the meal was prepared, Jesus sat at the table, joined by
the emissaries.

*T*he meal that Jesus and His disciples shared is still celebrated today among followers of Jesus. We surround it with varied
rituals and music, but the original meal took place in the midst of
great drama and tension. Next you'll hear the disciples arguing and
Jesus teaching them yet another lesson about life in the kingdom of
God. Jesus will speak of His own suffering and their betrayal and denial. Yet through it all, Jesus' focus remains on the central theme of
His life and mission: the coming of the kingdom of God.

Jesus | <sup>15</sup>It has been My deep desire to eat this Passover meal with you before My suffering begins. <sup>16</sup>Know this: I will not eat another Passover meal until its meaning is fulfilled in the kingdom of God.

<sup>17</sup>He took a cup *of wine* and gave thanks for it.

Jesus | Take this; share it among yourselves. <sup>18</sup>Know this: I will not drink another sip of wine until the kingdom of God has arrived in fullness.

<sup>19</sup>Then He took bread, gave thanks, broke it, and shared it with them.

Jesus | This is My body, My body given for you. Do this to remember Me.

<sup>20</sup>And similarly, after the meal had been eaten, He took the cup.

Jesus | This cup, which is poured out for you, is the new covenant, made in My blood. <sup>21</sup>But even now, the hand of My betrayer is with Me on this table. <sup>22</sup>As it has been determined, the Son of Man, *that firstfruit of a new generation of humanity,* must be betrayed, but how pitiful it will be for the person who betrays Him.

<sup>23</sup>They immediately began questioning each other.

**Disciples** | Which one of us could do such a horrible thing?

[24]Soon they found themselves arguing about the opposite question.

**Disciples** | Which one of us is the most faithful, the most important?

**Jesus**
*(interrupting)* | [25]The authority figures of the outsiders play this game, flexing their muscles in competition for power over one another, masking their quest for domination behind words like "benefactor" or "public servant." [26]But you must not indulge in this charade. Instead, among you, the greatest must become like the youngest and the leader must become a true servant. [27]Who is greater right here as we eat this meal—those of us who sit at the table, or those who serve us? Doesn't everyone normally assume those who are served are greater than those who serve? But consider My role among you. I have been with you as a servant.

[28]You have stood beside Me faithfully through My trials. [29]I give you a kingdom, just as the Father has given Me a kingdom. [30]You will eat and drink at My table in My kingdom, and you will have authority over the twelve tribes of Israel.

[31]Simon, Simon, how Satan has pursued you, that he might make you part of his harvest. [32]But I have prayed for you. I have prayed that your faith

will hold firm and that you will recover from your failure and become a source of strength for your brothers here.

Peter | *³³Lord, what are you talking about?* I'm going all the way to the end with You—to prison, to execution— *I'm prepared to do anything for You.*

Jesus | ³⁴No, Peter, the truth is that before the rooster crows at dawn, you will have denied that you even know Me, not just once, but three times. ³⁵Remember when I sent you out with no money, no pack, not even sandals? Did you lack anything?

Disciples | Not a thing.

Jesus | ³⁶It's different now. If you have some savings, take them with you. If you have a pack, *fill it and* bring it. If you don't have a sword, sell your coat and buy one. ³⁷Here's the truth: what the Hebrew Scriptures said, "And He was taken as one of the criminals,"* must come to fruition in Me. These words must come true.

Disciples | ³⁸Look, Lord, we have two swords here.

Jesus | That's enough.

---

**22:37** Isaiah 53:12

<sup>39</sup>Once again He left the city as He had been doing during recent days, returning to Mount Olivet along with His disciples.

*T*here is a powerful consistency in Jesus' life. Again and again we see Him withdraw from the crowds to pray in solitude. Now, at this dramatic moment, Jesus again withdraws to pray—in a solitude made more intense by the fact that He has asked His disciples to pray too; but they have fallen asleep. And in this moment of anguished emotion, we also hear on Jesus' lips a prayer that resonates with His consistent message of the Kingdom. He has taught His disciples to pray, "May Your kingdom come," which is a request for God's will to be done on earth as it is in heaven. Now, drenched in sweat, Jesus Himself prays simply for God's will to be done, even if it means that He must drink the cup of suffering that awaits Him in the hours ahead. We often speak of having faith *in* Jesus; but we seldom speak of the faith *of* Jesus, a faith that is demonstrated consistently throughout His life and now, here, in this place. In a moment of agony, Jesus still trusts God, still yields His will to God, and still approaches God as "Father," placing Himself in the position of a child, in trust—profound, tested, sincere.

<sup>40</sup>And He came to a certain place.

> **Jesus** | Pray for yourselves, that you will not sink into temptation.

<sup>41</sup>He distanced Himself from them about a stone's throw and knelt there, <sup>42</sup>praying.

**Jesus** | Father, if You are willing, take this cup away from Me. Yet not My will, but Your will, be done.

[⁴³Then a messenger from heaven appeared to strengthen Him. ⁴⁴And in His anguish He prayed even more intensely, and His sweat was like drops of blood falling to the ground.]* ⁴⁵When He rose from prayer and returned to the disciples, He found them asleep, weighed down with sorrow. ⁴⁶He roused them.

**Jesus** | Why are you sleeping? Wake up and pray that you will not sink into temptation.

⁴⁷Even as He said these words, *the sound of a crowd could be heard in the distance,* and as the crowd came into view, it was clear that Judas was leading them. He came close to Jesus and gave Jesus *the traditional greeting of* a kiss.

**Jesus** | ⁴⁸Ah, Judas, is this how you betray the Son of Man—with a kiss?

**Disciples** | ⁴⁹Lord, is this why You told us to bring the swords?
*(realizing what was going on)* | Should we attack?

⁵⁰Before Jesus could answer, one of them had swung his sword at the high priest's slave, cutting off his right ear.

**Jesus** | ⁵¹Stop! No more of this!

**22:43-44** Some ancient manuscripts omit verses 43-44.

Then He reached out to touch—and heal—the man's ear. [52]Jesus turned to the chief priests, the captains of the temple, and the elders and spoke.

**Jesus** | Do you think I'm some sort of violent criminal? Is that why you came with swords and clubs? [53]I haven't been hard to find—each day I've been in the temple in broad daylight, and you never tried to seize Me there. But this is your time—*night*—and this is your power—the power of darkness.

[54]They grabbed Him at this point and took Him away to the high priest's home. Peter followed—at a distance. [55]He *watched from the shadows as* those who had seized Jesus made a fire in the center of the courtyard and sat down around it. Then Peter *slipped in quietly and* sat with them. [56]But a young servant girl saw his face in the firelight. She stared for a while and then spoke.

**Servant Girl** | This fellow here was with Jesus. *I recognize him.*

**Peter**
*(denying it)* | [57]Woman, I don't even know the man.

[58]A little later, a man also recognized him.

**Man** | *I recognize you.* You're one of Jesus' followers.

**Peter** | Man, you're wrong. I'm not.

[59]An hour or so passed, and then another person pointed to Peter.

**Another Person** | This fellow is obviously Galilean. He must be a member of Jesus' group.

**Peter** | ⁶⁰Look, I have no idea what you're talking about.

And he hadn't even finished the sentence when a nearby rooster crowed. ⁶¹The Lord turned toward Peter, and their eyes met. Peter remembered Jesus' words about his triple denial before the rooster would crow, ⁶²so he left the courtyard and wept bitter tears.

⁶³At this point, the men who were holding Jesus began to mock Him and beat Him. ⁶⁴They put a blindfold on Him.

**Men holding Jesus** | *Hey, Prophet!* Use your prophetic powers to tell us who just whacked You!

⁶⁵They kept on with this sort of insulting, degrading treatment for quite some time. ⁶⁶When dawn had given way to full day, the Sanhedrin council assembled, consisting of religious leaders *of the Sadducean party*, along with the chief priests and religious scholars. They took Him to their headquarters *for interrogation*.

**Sanhedrin** | ⁶⁷If you are the Liberating King whom God promised us, tell us plainly.

**Jesus** | If I give you an answer, you won't believe it. ⁶⁸And if I ask you a question, you won't answer it. ⁶⁹But *this I will say to you:* from now on, the Son of Man will take His seat at the right hand of the power of God.

**Sanhedrin** | [70]So You are the Son of God, then?

**Jesus** | It's as you say.

**Sanhedrin** | [71]What more evidence do we need? We've heard it with our own ears from His own lips.

## FORGIVE THEM

¹So the whole council got up and took Jesus to Pilate. ²They brought accusations against Him.

**Sanhedrin** | We have observed this man leading our nation astray. He even forbade us to pay our taxes to Caesar. He claims to be the Liberator and a King Himself.

**Pilate** | ³Are You the King of the Jews?

**Jesus** | It's as you say.

**Pilate**
*(to the chief priest and crowd)* | ⁴I find this man guilty of no crime.

**Sanhedrin**
*(growing more intense)* | ⁵He has been stirring up discontent among the people all over Judea. He started up in Galilee, and now He's brought His brand of trouble all the way to Jerusalem!

**Pilate** | ⁶*Just a minute.* Is this man a Galilean?

⁷When Pilate learned *that Jesus was indeed Galilean*—which meant He was officially under Herod's jurisdiction—Pilate sent Him over to Herod, who was currently in Jerusalem. ⁸Herod was fascinated to

meet Jesus for he had heard about Him for a long time. He was hoping he might be treated to a miracle or two. [9]He interrogated Jesus for quite a while, but Jesus remained silent, refusing to answer his questions. [10]Meanwhile, the chief priests and religious scholars had plenty to say—angrily hurling accusations at Jesus.

[11]Eventually Herod and his soldiers began to insult Jesus, mocking and degrading Him. They put expensive clothing on Him and sent Him back to Pilate. [12]This ended a longstanding rift between Herod and Pilate; they became friends from that day forward.

[13]Pilate assembled the chief priests and other Jewish authorities.

**Pilate** | [14]You presented this man to me as a rabble-rouser, but I examined Him in your presence and found Him not guilty of the charges you have leveled against Him. [15]Herod also examined Him and released Him to my custody. So He hasn't done anything deserving the death penalty. [16]I'll see to it that He is properly whipped and then let Him go.

[17][It was the custom for Pilate to set one prisoner free during the holiday festivities.]*

**Crowd**
*(all shouting at once)* | [18]Away with this man! Free Barabbas instead!

[19]Barabbas had been imprisoned after being convicted of an insurrection he had led in Jerusalem. He had also committed murder.

---

**23:17** The earliest manuscripts omit verse 17.

²⁰Pilate argued with them, wishing he could release Jesus, ²¹but they wouldn't be silenced.

**Crowd** | Crucify Him! Crucify Him!
*(shouting)* |

**Pilate** | ²²Why? What has He done that is so evil? I have
*(countering a* | found in Him no offense worthy of capital punish-
*third time)* | ment. As I said, I will punish Him and then release
| Him.

²³But they would not relent. They shouted louder and louder that He should be crucified, and eventually Pilate capitulated. ²⁴So he pronounced the punishment they demanded.

²⁵He released the rebel and murderer *Barabbas*—the insurrectionist they had pleaded for in His place—and he handed Jesus over to them to do with as they desired.

²⁶On the way to the place of crucifixion, they pulled a man from the crowd—his name was Simon of Cyrene, a person from the countryside who happened to be entering the city at that moment. They put Jesus' cross on Simon's shoulders, and he followed behind Jesus. ²⁷Along with Him was a huge crowd of common people, including many women shrieking and wailing in grief.

**Jesus** | ²⁸Daughters of Jerusalem, do not weep for Me. Weep
*(to the people in* | instead for yourselves and weep for your children.
*the crowd)* | ²⁹Days are coming when people will say, "Blessed are
| the infertile, blessed are the wombs that never bore
| *a child*, blessed are the breasts that never nursed *an*
| *infant*." ³⁰People will beg the mountains, "Surround

us!" They'll plead with the hills, "Cover us!"* ³¹For if they treat Me like this when I'm like green unseasoned wood, what will they do to a nation that's ready to burn like seasoned firewood?

³²*Jesus wasn't the only one being crucified that day.* There were two others, criminals, who were also being led to their execution. ³³When they came to the place known as "The Skull," they crucified Jesus there, in the company of criminals, one to the right of Jesus and the other to His left.

*H*istorians tell us that crucifixion was often used for insurrectionists. Anyone who dared to defy the power and authority of Caesar would be executed in this public and humiliating way. The cross, then, became a symbol of the invincible and dominating power of Caesar and his empire; and Jesus is crucified as a revolutionary, between two other revolutionaries. The ironies are powerful.

First, Jesus indeed was a revolutionary. He didn't come to proclaim a new religion, but a new kingdom—a new way of life. He was indeed a threat to Caesar's way of doing things, a way that had co-opted the religious leaders. But Jesus wasn't a threat in the way His neighbors on the other two crosses were a threat, which brings us to the second irony: Jesus' revolution was a peaceful revolution.

Jesus didn't advocate the use of violence—in fact, a few hours earlier, when one of His disciples used the sword to try to protect

Jesus from arrest, Jesus healed the "enemy" and rebuked His disciple. So Jesus doesn't support the regime of Caesar on the one hand,
but on the other hand, He doesn't follow the usual violent path of
revolution: He leads a revolutionary revolution—in a path of love,
healing, justice, and reconciliation.

Third, instead of being humiliated and defeated by the cross,
Jesus appropriates the cross from Rome. He transforms the symbol
of their power into a symbol of His greater power. He makes it, not
the icon of violent domination, but the reverse. By hanging on the
cross and speaking of forgiveness, Jesus shows that there is a
greater power at work in the world than the power of domination:
it's the power of God's saving and reconciling love.

**Jesus** | [³⁴Father, forgive them, for they don't know what
they're doing.]*

Meanwhile, they were throwing dice to see who would win Jesus'
clothing. ³⁵The crowd of people stood, watching.

**Authorities** | So He was supposed to rescue others, was He? He
*(mocking Jesus)* | was supposed to be the big Liberator from God,
God's special Messenger? Let's see Him start by liberating Himself!

³⁶The soldiers joined in the mockery. First, they *pretended to offer
Him a soothing drink*—but it was sour wine.

---

23:34 The earliest manuscripts omit verse 34.

**Soldiers** | ³⁷Hey, if You're the King of the Jews, why don't You free Yourself!

³⁸Even the inscription they placed over Him was intended to mock Him—"This is the King of the Jews!" [This was written in Greek, Latin, and Hebrew.]*

³⁹One of the criminals joined in the cruel talk.

**Cynical Criminal** | You're supposed to be the Liberator, right? *Well—do it!* Rescue Yourself and us!

⁴⁰But the other criminal told him to be quiet.

**Believing Criminal** | Don't you have any fear of God at all? You're getting the same death sentence He is! ⁴¹We're getting what we deserve since we've committed crimes, but this man hasn't done anything wrong at all! (turning to Jesus) ⁴²Jesus, when You come into Your kingdom, please remember me.

**Jesus** | ⁴³I promise you that this very day you will be with Me in paradise.

⁴⁴At this point, it was about noon, and a darkness fell over the whole region. The darkness persisted until about three in the afternoon, ⁴⁵and at some point during this darkness, the curtain in the temple was torn in two.

---

**23:38** Some ancient manuscripts omit the end of verse 38.

*T*he tearing of this heavy curtain in the temple is highly symbolic. Because this curtain separated the holiest place in the temple from the rest of the temple, some have seen in this act a symbol of God opening the way for unholy humans to enter into His holy presence: Jesus' death has brought forgiveness and opened the way for all to come to God. Others have seen in the curtain's being torn the opposite meaning: God's presence can no longer be confined to any single geographical place. The suffering and death of Jesus ended one age of human history, and now a new era has begun. Now God is on the move, at large, invading the whole world. Or perhaps, this graphic image could mean both.

**Jesus**
*(shouting out loudly)*

⁴⁶Father, I entrust My spirit into Your hands!*

And with those words, He exhaled—and breathed no more.

⁴⁷The Centurion—*one of the soldiers who performed the execution*—saw all this, and he praised God.

**Centurion** | No doubt, this man must have been innocent.

⁴⁸The crowds of common people who had gathered and watched the whole ordeal through to its conclusion left for their homes, pounding on their own chests *in profound grief.* ⁴⁹And all who knew Jesus personally, including the group of women who had been with

Him *from the beginning* in Galilee, stood at a distance, watching all of these things unfold.

[50]Meanwhile, a man named Joseph *had been at work.* He was a member of the council, a good and fair man, [51]from a Judean town called Arimathea. He had objected to the plans and actions of the council; he was seeking the kingdom of God. [52]He had gone to Pilate and asked for the body of Jesus. [53]He removed the body from the cross and wrapped it in a shroud made of *fine* linen. He then laid the body in a cavelike tomb cut from solid rock, a tomb that never had been used before. [54]It was Preparation Day—*the day before the holiday*—and the special Sabbath was about to begin *at sundown.* [55]The women who had accompanied Jesus *from the beginning* in Galilee now came, took note of where the tomb was and how His body had been prepared, [56]then left to prepare spices and ointments *for His proper burial.* They ceased their work on the Sabbath so they could rest as the *Hebrew* Scriptures required.

## HE OPENED THEIR MINDS

¹Early on Sunday morning, even before the sun had fully risen, these women made their way back to the tomb with the spices *and ointments* they had prepared. ²When they arrived, they found the stone was rolled away from the tomb entrance, ³and when they looked inside, the body of the Lord Jesus was nowhere to be seen. ⁴They didn't know what to think. As they stood there in confusion, two men suddenly appeared standing beside them. These men seemed to glow with light. ⁵The women were so terrified that they fell to the ground facedown.

**Two Men** | Why are you seeking the living One in the place of the dead? ⁶He is not here. He has risen *from the dead.* Don't you remember what He told you way back in Galilee? ⁷He told you that the Son of Man must be handed over to wicked men, He must be crucified, and then on the third day He must rise.

*T*his phrase, "Son of Man," is very important in Luke's story; but scholars struggle to capture its many layers of meaning. It could mean "epitome of humanity" or "prime example of what a human can be." But it also evokes a specific passage of Scripture that was very important to Jewish people of Jesus' day, Daniel 7:13-27. There, the phrase "Son of Man" refers to a king who receives an eternal and universal kingdom, and it also represents "the saints of the Most High"—the people of God. In light of Jesus' central message about the kingdom of God, it seems likely that the phrase should suggest to us that Jesus is the long-awaited Liberating King who launches a new era in human history and who creates a community of people who will represent the eternal and universal kingdom of God. In this way, "Son of" suggests "new generation of" and "Man" suggests "humanity." Jesus is Himself the new generation of humanity (a second Adam, a new beginning), and the community He creates will also share this identity (a new creation, a new humanity in Christ). The two messengers here use this pregnant phrase in a way that would have shocked everyone: The way this long-awaited Liberating King would receive His kingdom would not be through conventional military victory where enemies were defeated and killed. No, this King would receive His kingdom by suffering, dying, and rising again Himself. Amazing news—good news!

[8]The women did remember Jesus' words about this, [9]so they returned from the tomb and found the eleven and recounted for them—and others with them—everything they had experienced. [10-11]The emissaries heard their stories as fiction, a lie; they didn't believe a word of it. (By the way, this group of women included Mary Magdalene, Joanna, and Mary the mother of James, along with a number of others.) [12]Peter, however, got up and ran to the tomb. *When he reached the opening,* he bent down, looked inside, and saw the linen burial cloths lying there. But the body was gone. He walked away, full of wonder about what had happened.

¹³*Picture this:*

That same day, two other disciples *(not of the eleven)* are traveling the seven miles from Jerusalem to Emmaus. ¹⁴As they walk along, they talk back and forth about all that has transpired during recent days. ¹⁵While they're talking, discussing, and conversing, Jesus catches up to them and begins walking with them, ¹⁶but for some reason they don't recognize Him.

Jesus | ¹⁷*You two seem deeply engrossed in conversation. What are you talking about as you walk along this road?*

They stop walking and just stand there, looking sad. ¹⁸One of them—Cleopas is his name—speaks up.

Cleopas | You must be the only visitor in Jerusalem who hasn't heard about what's been going on over the last few days.

Jesus | ¹⁹What are you talking about?

Two Disciples | It's all about the man named Jesus of Nazareth. He was a powerful prophet who did amazing miracles and preached powerful messages in the sight of God and everyone around. ²⁰Our chief priests and authorities handed Him over to be executed—crucified, in fact.

²¹We had been hoping that He was the One—you know, the One who would liberate all Israel and bring God's promised work. Anyway, on top of all this, just this morning—the third day after the execution—²²some women in our group really shocked us. They went to the tomb early this morning, ²³but they didn't see His body anywhere. Then they came back and told us they did see something—a vision of heavenly messengers—and these messengers said that Jesus was alive. ²⁴Some people in our group went to the tomb to check it out, and just as the women had said, it was empty. But they didn't see Jesus.

Jesus | ²⁵Come on, men! Why are you being so foolish? Why are your hearts so sluggish when it comes to believing what the prophets have been saying all along? ²⁶Didn't it have to be this way? Didn't the Liberating King have to experience these sufferings in order to come into His glory?

²⁷Then He begins with Moses and continues, prophet by prophet, explaining the meaning of the Hebrew Scriptures, showing how they were talking about the very things that had happened to Jesus.

²⁸About this time they are nearing their destination,

Jesus keeps walking ahead as if He has no plans to stop there, [29]but they convince Him to join them.

**Two Disciples** | Please, be our guest. It's getting late, and soon it will be too dark to walk.

So He accompanies them to their home. [30]When they sit down at the table for dinner, He takes the bread in His hands, He gives thanks for it, and then He breaks it and hands it to them. [31]At that instant, *two things happen simultaneously:* their eyes are suddenly opened so they recognize Him, and He instantly vanishes—just disappears before their eyes.

**Two Disciples**
*(to each other)* | [32]*Amazing!* Weren't our hearts on fire within us while He was talking to us on the road? *Didn't you feel it all coming clear* as He explained the meaning of the Hebrew Scriptures?

[33]So they get up immediately and rush back to Jerusalem—*all seven miles*—where they find the eleven gathered together—the eleven plus a number of others. [34]*Before Cleopas and his companion can tell their story,* the others have their own story to tell.

**Other Disciples** | The Lord has risen indeed! It's true! He appeared to Simon!

[35]Then the two men report their own experience—their conversation along the road, their moment of realization and

recognition as He broke the bread. [36]At that very instant, as they're still telling the story, Jesus is there, standing there among them!

> **Jesus** | May you have peace!

[37]*You might expect them to be overjoyed, but they aren't.* They're startled and terrified; they think they're seeing a ghost.

> **Jesus** | [38]Why are you upset? Why are your hearts churning with questions? [39]Look—look at My hands and My feet! See that it's Me! Come on; touch Me; see for yourselves. A ghost doesn't have flesh and bones, as you can see that I have!

[40]Then He shows them His hands and His feet.*
[41]Now their fear gives way to joy, but it seems too good to be true and they're still unsure.

> **Jesus** | Do you have anything here to eat?

[42]They hand Him a piece of broiled fish, [43]and He takes it and eats it in front of them.

> **Jesus** | [44]I've been telling you this all along, that everything written about Me in the Hebrew Scriptures must be fulfilled—everything

---

**24:40** Some manuscripts omit this verse.

from the law of Moses to the prophets to
the psalms.

⁴⁵Then He opens their minds so they can comprehend
the meaning of the Hebrew Scriptures.

**Jesus** | ⁴⁶This is what the Scriptures said: that the
promised Liberating King should suffer and
rise from the dead on the third day, ⁴⁷that in
His name a radical change of thought and
life should be preached, and that in His
name the forgiveness of sins should be
preached, beginning in Jerusalem and ex-
tending to all nations. ⁴⁸You have witnessed
the fulfillment of these things. ⁴⁹So I am
sending My Father's promise to you. Stay in
the city until you receive it—until power
from heaven comes upon you.

⁵⁰Then He leads them out to Bethany. He lifts up His
hands and blesses them, ⁵¹and at that moment, with His
hands raised in blessing, He leaves them and is carried up
into heaven. They worship Him, then they return to
Jerusalem, filled with intense joy, ⁵³and they return again and
again to the temple to celebrate God.

*L*uke has told his story. It ends with joy and praise. The
crucified Jesus has been resurrected and has ascended to heaven to

take His place at God's right hand just as the ancient prophets predicted. For the band of disciples, Easter joy has eclipsed Good Friday sorrow.

This ending point becomes the starting point for Luke's sequel, known to us as "The Acts of the Apostles." You see, the story isn't really over; it's just begun. The life and ministry of Jesus that Luke has just recounted is the mustard-seed stage of the kingdom of God that continues to grow and grow and grow. Now it's time for this Kingdom to fill the world. If the Gospel we have just read is about what Jesus began to do and teach, then Luke's sequel will tell us what the risen Jesus continued to do and teach through His followers. And of course, that story continues to today. In fact, Luke writes in hope that our lives can be taken up into this beautiful story that will never, ever end.

Section Two // excerpts from

*The Last Eyewitness*

*The Dust Off Their Feet*

and

*The Voice of Matthew*

# Chapter 2

## Learning to Serve

My name is John. My father's name was Zebedee. We made our living by fishing on the Sea of Galilee. I am the last eyewitness to the life of Jesus. All the rest are gone, some long gone. Many died years ago, tragically young, the victims of Roman cruelty and persecution. For some reason Jesus chose me to live to be an old man. In fact, some in my community have taken to calling me "the elder." I suppose that's because there are others with the name "John" in our community.

I am the inspiration behind the Fourth Gospel. These are my stories, recorded, told to you by my disciples. I'm proud of what they have done. Me? I've never done much writing. But the story is truly mine.

You see my hands. They've been hurting for the past 20 years now. I couldn't hold a pen even if I wanted to. Not that I was ever good at writing. I was a fisherman so my hands were calloused. I could tie ropes, mend nets, and pull the oars, but never make a decent *xi* (Greek letter). So we used secretaries when we wanted to write. There was always a bright young man around it seems, ready to take a letter or help us put pen to papyrus. Even our brother Paul used secretaries—Tertius, Luke, and Titus—just to name a few.

John the Evangelist

My eyes are too weak to read anymore. I can't remember the last time I could see well enough to read a letter or even see the inscriptions. So one of the brothers (I call them, "my little children") reads to me. They are all very gracious to me in my old age, compiling my stories, bringing me food, laughing at my jokes, and caring for my most intimate needs. Time is taking its toll on me though. I rarely have the energy to tell the old stories and preach entire sermons. Instead, I simply remind them of Christ's most vital command, saying as loudly as I can, "Little children, love one another." I repeat this phrase quite often.

Jesus had this group of guys. He called us "the twelve." We traveled with Him, spent time with Him, ate with Him, and listened to Him talk about God's kingdom. We watched Him perform miracles. These weren't the tricks like you see in the market or attempts at magic you hear about at shrines. These were what I call signs. Something was breaking into our darkness. These signs pointed to a greater reality most people didn't even know was there. In the other Gospels they call them miracles or works of power. We've decided to tell you about select signs because these, more than any, revealed the true glory of this Man.

Jesus wanted us to be His family, a different kind of community. We figured it out later. By calling us "the twelve," Jesus was creating a new people of God. God was doing something new, like the prophets had promised. We were living at the center of history. From now on everything would be different. This made us feel special, proud, and sometimes arrogant. We'd sometimes jockey for Jesus' attention. Even within "the twelve" some were closer to Jesus. He had this "inner circle" of sorts. I was part of it. Peter, Andrew, James, and I were with Jesus at times when the other fellows had to stay behind. I'm not sure why He picked me. Because of that, I knew He loved me and I would have a special place with Him.

Jesus also had other students. Not all of them stayed. Some came and some went. I don't really know how many people in all. One time He sent out seventy of us to proclaim the good news and heal in His name. He even let women be His students. Most people don't know this, but women were among those who helped support us financially (Lk 8). At a time when people said it was a shame for a man to be supported by women, Jesus took their help and took it gladly. For Him it was like a badge of honor. But there were no women among "the twelve." That was only right. In our day women didn't travel with men who were not family. Scandal was always swirling around Jesus; He didn't want or need to fight that battle.

I've outlived all the rest of "the twelve" and His other followers. I can't tell you how lonely it is to be the last person with a memory, some would even say a fuzzy memory, of what Jesus looked like, the sound of His voice, the manner of His walk, the penetrating look in His eyes. All I can do is tell my story.

The Scripture says God knows the length of our days. Jesus reminded us that the Eternal has the hairs of our head numbered and knows when a little bird drops from the sky. So He knows how this feeble body aches. The mornings are the worst times.

I used to sleep—one of the benefits of a clean conscience, I suppose. But I don't sleep much anymore. Now these memories fill my thoughts. I constantly think about all those experiences of being with Jesus each day. So at night I think, I remember, I pray, I wait. I still look for His coming.

Some brothers have criticized me for my hope in His coming. They say that this is all that there is. What we have, of course, is great—the Spirit is strong with us, we have a vibrant community, God does things among us no one can explain—but still, I know there is more. I've seen it in His eyes. Oh, there's so much more.

So I wait.

Others criticize me for neglecting the blessed hope of His coming. I can't win. Because I speak so passionately of God's blessings now and how the Kingdom is with us now, some accuse me of forgetting about His coming. Nothing could be further from the truth.

Those of us who walked with Jesus were like most Jews in my village. We expected the Messiah to field an army, face off with the Romans, and reestablish the glory days of David and Solomon. We were completely disarmed by the simplicity and power of Jesus' voice, of His message. Only after the resurrection did the full weight settle in of what He said.

Before Jesus came along, many thought John the Immerser might be the Messiah. But when Jesus appeared in the wilderness, John pointed us to Him. The Immerser knew his place in God's redemptive plan. But there are still those who think he was more significant than Jesus. That movement is especially vocal in Ephesus. I feel like it is important for me to set the record straight. John the Immerser was a man sent from God. But Jesus is the Voice of God. John rejected any messianic claim outright. Jesus, though, accepted it with a smile, but only from a few of us—at least at first. Don't get me wrong, John was important, but he wasn't the Messiah. He preached repentance. He told us we were flawed—seriously flawed and we needed God's help. So he told everybody to get ready for One greater to come along. The One who comes will immerse us in fire and power, he said. John even told some of his followers to leave him and go follow Jesus.

Others have written accounts of what happened among us. I'd like to hear what they all have had to say. The ones I have heard have done a good job. But I have stories to tell no one is talking about. The other Gospels have faithfully portrayed the public Jesus. But I feel compelled to tell the story of the private Jesus. The others show us how Jesus preached and dealt with the multitudes. But I still remember the small group time with Jesus and the conversations that Jesus had with Nicodemus, the Samaritan woman, and the man born blind—I don't remember his name.

The other Gospels tell the tragedy and injustice of Jesus' death. Here was the single greatest man in history who was falsely accused; who was dragged before corrupt priests and a cruel Roman governor. He was condemned to death and crucified in a most hideous manner. On a human level, Jesus' arrest, condemnation, and crucifixion was a tragedy of epic proportions. But the more this old man thinks about what happened, the more I understand now that Jesus' death was His greatest hour. Things seemed to spin out of control so quickly. One minute we were celebrating the Passover together in the upper room; the next we were running for our lives! I'm not sure who was to blame for what happened to Jesus. Envious priests. The Roman governor. But, in fact, He was in complete control. That's why I say the hour of His death was the hour of His greatest glory. That's why I think that when Jesus was lifted up on the cross, He became the means by which all people can come to God. The most vivid memory that lingers in this old man's mind is of Jesus up there, on the cross. I can still see it like it was yesterday. His body—hanging halfway between heaven and earth, embracing the world—bridged the gap between God and humanity.

But I am getting way ahead of myself. There is one part of this fascinating story that I want to tell you about right now. Of all the things this old man has seen in his many years, the things that we saw and heard that week were the most startling.

Now I want to be very clear. This is my story, but unlike what you hear from most storytellers, this is completely true. I am giving you the testimony of an eyewitness. And like my brother disciples, I will swear upon my life that it is true.

## John 13

¹Before the Passover festival began, Jesus was keenly aware that His hour had come to depart from this world and to return to the Father. From beginning to end, Jesus' days were marked by His love for His people. ²Before Jesus and His disciples gathered for dinner, the adversary filled Judas Iscariot's heart with plans of deceit and betrayal. ³Jesus, knowing that He had come from God and was going away to God, ⁴stood up from dinner and removed His outer garments. He then wrapped Himself in a towel, ⁵poured water in a basin, and began to wash the feet of the disciples, drying them with His towel.

| | | |
|---|---|---|
| **Simon Peter** | 6 | *(as Jesus approaches)* Lord, are You going to wash my feet? |
| **Jesus** | 7 | Peter, you don't realize what I am doing, but you will understand later. |
| **Peter** | 8 | You will not wash my feet, now or ever! |

---

I have to interrupt the story so you can get the whole picture. Can you imagine what it would feel like to have Jesus (the creative force behind the entire cosmos) wash your feet?

Have you ever been in a gathering where a rich and powerful person offers to fill your glass? You are thinking, "I should do this myself. How is it that someone of your stature would be willing to serve me?" But later you find yourself serving those who would view you as rich and powerful in the same ways that you were

Jesus Washing the Disciples' Feet

served. Multiply that experience by thousands, and you will have a small glimpse of this powerful expression.

My life changed that day; there was a new clarity about how I was supposed to live. I saw the world in a totally new way. The dirt, grime, sin, pain, rebellion, and torment around me were no longer an impediment to the spiritual path—it was the path.

Where I saw pain and filth, I found an opportunity to extend God's kingdom through an expression of love, humility, and service. This simple act is a metaphor for the lens that Christ gives us to see the cosmos. He sees the people, the world He created—which He loves—He sees the filth, the corruption in the world that torments us. His mission is to cleanse those whom He loves from the horrors that torment them. This is His redemptive work with feet, families, disease, famine, and our hearts.

So many of you have missed the heart of the gospel and Christ's example. When you see sin exposed in people, you shake your head and think how sad it is. Or worse you look down at these people for their rejection of God, lack of understanding, and poor morals. This is not the way of Christ. When Christ saw disease, He saw the opportunity to heal. Where He saw sin, He saw a chance to forgive and redeem. When He saw dirty feet, He saw a chance to wash them.

What do you see when you wander through the market, along the streets, on the beaches, and through the slums? Are you disgusted? Or do you seize the opportunity to expand God's reign of love in the cosmos? This is what Jesus did. The places we avoid, Jesus seeks. Now I must digress to tell a bit of the story from long before. I remember Him leading our little group of disciples into one of the most wretched places I have ever seen. It was a series of pools where the crippled and diseased would gather in hopes of being healed. The stench was unbearable, and no sane person would march into an area littered with wretched bodies and communicable diseases. We followed Him reluctantly as He approached a crippled man on his mat and said to him, "Are you here in this place hoping to be healed?" The disabled man responded, "Kind Sir, I wait, like all of these people for the waters to stir, but I cannot walk. If I am to be healed by the waters, some-one must carry me into the pool. So, the answer to Your question is yes—but I cannot be healed here unless someone will help me. Without a helping hand, someone else beats me to the water each time it is stirred." So, Jesus said, "Stand up, carry your mat and walk." At the moment Jesus uttered these words a healing energy coursed through the man and returned life to his limbs—he stood and walked for the first time in thirty-eight years (5:6-9).

It was not clear to us whether or not this man deserved this miracle. In fact, many of the disciples were disgusted by his lack of gratefulness and that he implicated Jesus to some of the Jewish authorities for healing him on the Sabbath. But God's grace is not earned; it is a beautiful gift to all of us.

When Jesus washed our feet He made an announcement to all who follow His path that life would not be about comfort, health, prosperity, and selfish pursuit.

I have gotten away from the story that was barely started. Let me back up and start almost from the beginning of the story again.

## John 13

| | | |
|---|---|---|
| **Simon Peter** | 6 | *(as Jesus approaches)* Lord, are You going to wash my feet? |
| **Jesus** | 7 | Peter, you don't realize what I am doing, but you will understand later. |
| **Peter** | 8 | You will not wash my feet, now or ever! |

| Jesus | | If I don't wash you, you will have nothing to do with Me. |
|---|---|---|
| Peter | 9 | Then wash me but don't stop with my feet. Cleanse my hands and head as well. |
| Jesus | 10 | Listen, anyone who has bathed is clean all over except for the feet. But I tell you this, not all of you are clean. |

[11]He knew the one with plans of betraying Him, which is why He said, "not all of you are clean." [12]After washing their feet and picking up His garments, He reclined at the table again.

| Jesus | | Do you understand what I have done to you? |
|---|---|---|
| | 13 | You call Me Teacher and Lord, and truly, that is |
| | 14 | who I am. So, if your Lord and Teacher washes your feet, then you should wash one another's |
| | 15 | feet. I am your example; keep doing what I do. |
| | 16 | I tell you the truth: an apostle is not greater than the master. Those who are sent are not greater |
| | 17 | than the One who sends them. If you know these things, and if you put them into practice, |
| | 18 | you will find happiness. I am not speaking about all of you. I know whom I have chosen, but let the Scripture be fulfilled that says, "The very same man who eats My bread with Me, will |
| | 19 | stab Me in the back." Assuredly, I tell you these truths before they happen, so that when it all |
| | 20 | transpires you will believe that I am. I tell you the truth: anyone who accepts the ones I send accepts Me. In turn, the ones who accept Me, also accept the One who sent Me. |

²¹Jesus was becoming visibly distressed.

| | |
|---|---|
| **Jesus** | I tell you the truth: one of you will betray Me. |

²²The disciples began to stare at one another, wondering who was the unfaithful disciple. ²³One disciple in particular, who was loved by Jesus, reclined next to Him at the table. ²⁴Peter motioned to the disciple at Jesus' side.

| | | |
|---|---|---|
| **Peter** | | *(to the beloved disciple)* Find out who the betrayer is. |
| **Beloved Disciple** | 25 | *(leaning in to Jesus)* Lord, who is it? |
| **Jesus** | 26 | I will dip a piece of bread in My cup and give it to the one who will betray Me. |

He dipped one piece in the cup and gave it to Judas, the son of Simon Iscariot. ²⁷After this occurred, Satan entered into Judas.

| | |
|---|---|
| **Jesus** | *(to Judas)* Make haste, and do what you are going to do. |

²⁸No one understood Jesus' instructions to Judas. ²⁹Because Judas carried the money, some thought he was being instructed to buy the necessary items for the feast, or give some money to the poor. ³⁰So Judas took his piece of bread and departed into the night.
³¹Upon Judas' departure, Jesus spoke:

| | | |
|---|---|---|
| **Jesus** | 32 | Now the Son of Man will be glorified as God is glorified in Him. If God's glory is in Him, His glory is also in God. The moment of this astounding |

| | | |
|---|---|---|
| | **33** | glory is imminent. My children, My time here is brief. You will be searching for Me, and as I told the Jews, "You cannot go where I am going." |
| | **34** | So, I give you a new command: Love each other deeply and fully. Remember the ways that I have loved you, and demonstrate your love for |
| | **35** | others in those same ways. Everyone will know you as followers of Christ if you demonstrate your love to others. |
| **Simon Peter** | **36** | Lord, where are You going? |
| **Jesus** | | Peter, you cannot come with Me now, but later you will join Me. |
| **Peter** | **37** | Why can't I go now? I'll give my life for You! |
| **Jesus** | **38** | Will you really give your life for Me? I tell you the truth: you will deny Me three times before the rooster crows. |

Ultimately, Peter was telling the truth. He was more than willing to lay down his life. But none of us understood the magnitude of the persecution and hatred that was about to be unleashed on all of us. You ask me, "Did that change the way you led and treated people in your community or outside of it? Some of us think you have an ax to grind with the Jews. What connection did this pattern of living have with Jesus' command to love? How can you reconcile your angst against the Jews and this command Christ gave you to love?"

# *Acts 1*

## CONTINUING THE JOURNEY

¹To *a lover of God,* Theophilus:

In my first book I recounted the events of Jesus' life—His actions, His teachings—²⁻³*from the beginning of His life* until He was taken up into heaven. After His great suffering *and vindication,* He showed His apostles that He was alive—appearing to them repeatedly over a period of 40 days, giving them many convincing proofs of His resurrection. As before, He spoke constantly of the kingdom of God. During these appearances, He had instructed His chosen messengers through the Holy Spirit, ⁴prohibiting them from leaving Jerusalem, but rather requiring them to wait there until they received what He called "the promise of the Father."

> **Jesus** | This is what you heard Me teach—⁵that just as John ritually cleansed* people with water, so you will be washed with the Holy Spirit very soon.

*S*cripture doesn't preserve Jesus' teachings during those mysterious meetings with the apostles after His death. We can only imagine the joy, curiosity, and amazement of the disciples as they hung on every word. What we do know is that His presence proved the reality of His bodily resurrection beyond any doubt and that He primarily wanted to talk to them about the kingdom of God. These words were

---

1:5 Literally, immersed, in a rite of initiation and purification

undoubtedly intended to prepare each of them for this journey, a journey with a clear destination in sight—the kingdom of God.

The kingdom of God is not a place, a belief system, a government, or a work of fiction—it's not even the heavenly kingdom. The kingdom of God is the rule of God in the hearts of His people. God is creating more than just the church out of this ragtag group of Christ-followers. He is birthing the kingdom of God, and the Holy Spirit is the midwife.

⁶When they had gathered *just outside Jerusalem at the Mount of Olives,* they asked Jesus,

> **Disciples** | Is now the time, Lord—the time when You will reestablish Your kingdom in our land of Israel?

> **Jesus** | ⁷The Father, on His own authority, has determined the ages and epochs of history, but you have not been given this knowledge. ⁸*Here's the knowledge you need:* you will receive power when the Holy Spirit comes on you. And you will be My witnesses, first here in Jerusalem, then beyond to Judea and Samaria, and finally to the farthest places on earth.

⁹As He finished this commission, He began to rise from the ground before their eyes until the clouds obscured Him from their vision. ¹⁰The apostles realized two men in white robes were standing among them.

> **Two Men** | ¹¹You Galileans, why are you standing here staring up into the sky? This Jesus who is leaving you and

ascending to heaven will return in the same way you
see Him departing.

[12]Then the disciples returned to Jerusalem—their short journey
from the Mount of Olives was an acceptable Sabbath Day's walk.

[13-14]Back in the city, they went to the room where they were stay-
ing—a second-floor room. This whole group devoted themselves to
constant prayer with one accord: Peter, John, James, Andrew, Philip,
Thomas, Bartholomew, Matthew, James (son of Alphaeus), Simon (the
Zealot), Judas (son of James), a number of women including Mary
(Jesus' mother), and some of Jesus' brothers.

[15]As the disciples prayed, Peter stood among the group of about 120
people and made this proposal:

**Peter** | [16-17]My friends, everything in the Hebrew Scriptures
had to be fulfilled, including what the Holy Spirit
foretold through David about Judas. *As you know,* Judas
was one of us and participated in our ministry until
he guided the authorities to arrest Jesus. [18](He was
paid handsomely for his betrayal, and he bought a field
with the blood money. But he died on that land—
falling so that his abdomen burst and his internal or-
gans gushed out. [19]News of this death spread to
everyone in Jerusalem, so Judas's property is known as
Hakeldama, which means "field of blood.") [20]In this way,
one of *David's* psalms was fulfilled: "May their camps
be bleak, with not one left in any tent."* But the psalm

---

1:20 Psalm 69:25-26

also includes these words: "Let his position of over-
sight be given to another."* [21]So we need to determine
his replacement from among the men who have been
with us during all of the Lord Jesus' travels among
us—[22]from His ritual cleansing* by John until His as-
cension. We need someone to join us as a witness of
Jesus' resurrection.

[23]The group put forward two men: Joseph (who was also known as
Barsabbas or Justus) and Matthias.

**Disciples** | [24]Lord, You know everyone's heart. Make it clear to us
which of these two is Your choice [25]to take on this
ministry as an apostle, replacing Judas who went his
own way to his own destination.

[26]Then they drew lots, and the lot fell to Matthias, so he was added
to the 11 apostles *to reconstitute the twelve.*

*T*he Creator of heaven and earth is orchestrating a redemptive
story that will radically change the course of history. The most significant supernatural event in the history of this newly formed church will
be the filling of the Holy Spirit. Through the Holy Spirit, God will direct
the church's growth. But how did the early church make important decisions before the Holy Spirit descended on them?
   With much thought and prayer?

---

**1:20** Psalm 109:8
**1:22** Literally, immersion, an act of repentance

By a carefully appointed committee?

With a democratic vote?

No. They left their decisions up to the providential leading of God. They called it "drawing lots." To seek God's direction, Joseph and Matthias most likely wrote their names on scraps; then someone drew the replacement's name out of a bag. What seems to us like a 50/50 chance was, in fact, God's way of imparting His will. You see, the disciples weren't putting their faith in "chance." They were putting their faith in a God who lives. And this living God wasn't distant; He was a player in their lives, active when His people sought Him and His will. They believed that God directed the process, start to finish, and determined whose name was drawn to join the eleven. When they drew lots, these early believers were using a centuries-old method to discern God's will. But with the filling of the Holy Spirit, the communication from God became more direct, and the drawing of lots was obsolete.

## A TASTE OF THE KINGDOM

¹When the holy day of Pentecost came *50 days after Passover*, they were gathered together in one place.

*Picture yourself among the disciples:* ²A sound roars from the sky without warning, the roar of a violent wind, and the whole house where you are gathered reverberates with the sound. ³Then a flame appears, dividing into smaller flames and spreading from one person to the next. ⁴All the apostles are filled with the Holy Spirit and begin speaking in languages they've never spoken, as the Spirit empowers them.

⁵*Because of the holiday,* there were devoted Jews staying as pilgrims in Jerusalem from every nation under the sun. ⁶They heard the sound, and a crowd gathered. They were amazed because each of them could hear the group speaking in their native languages. ⁷They were shocked and amazed by this.

**Pilgrims** | Just a minute. Aren't all of these people Galileans? ⁸How in the world do we all hear our native languages being spoken? ⁹*Look*—there are Parthians *here*, and Medes, Elamites, Mesopotamians, and Judeans, residents of Cappadocia, Pontus, and Asia, ¹⁰Phrygians and Pamphylians, Egyptians and Libyans from Cyrene, Romans including both Jews by birth and converts, ¹¹Cretans, and Arabs. We're each, in our own languages, hearing these people talk about God's powerful deeds.

[12]Their amazement became confusion as they wondered,

**Pilgrims** | What does this mean?

**Skeptics** | [13]It doesn't mean anything. They're all drunk on some fresh wine!

*N*o matter who you were or what you may have seen, this miraculous sign of God's kingdom would have astounded you. The followers of Jesus were not known as people who drank too much wine with breakfast, but this unusual episode required some kind of explanation. Unfortunately, we can't comprehend or express what transpired on Pentecost. But this was not a novelty performance; rather, it was a taste of the kingdom of God.

[14]As the twelve stood together, Peter shouted to the crowd,

**Peter** | Men of Judea and all who are staying here in Jerusalem, listen. I want you to understand: [15]these people aren't drunk as you may think. Look, it's only nine o'clock in the morning! [16]*No, this isn't drunkenness;* this is the fulfillment of the prophecy of Joel. [17]*Hear what God says!*

In the last days, I will offer My Spirit to humanity as a libation.
Your children will boldly speak *the word of the Lord.*

Young warriors will see visions, and your elders will
dream dreams.

[18]Yes, in those days I shall offer My Spirit to all servants,
Both male and female, [and they will boldly speak the
word of the Lord].

[19]And in the heaven above and on the earth below,
I shall give signs *of impending judgment*: blood, fire, and
clouds of smoke.

[20]The sun will become a void of darkness, and the moon
will become blood.

Then the great and dreadful day of the Lord will arrive,

[21]And everyone who pleads using the name of the Lord
Will be liberated *into God's freedom and peace*.*

[22]All of you Israelites, listen to my message: it's about
Jesus of Nazareth, a Man whom God authenticated for
you by performing in your presence powerful deeds,
wonders, and signs through Him, just as you yourselves
know. [23]This *Man, Jesus*, who came into your hands by
God's sure plan and advanced knowledge, you nailed to
a cross and killed in collaboration with lawless Gentiles.
[24]But God raised Jesus and unleashed Him from the ago-
nizing birth-pains of death, for death could not possibly
keep Jesus in its power. [25]David spoke *of Jesus'*
*resurrection*, saying:

The Lord is ever present with me. I will not live in
fear or abandon my calling because He guides my

right hand. <sup>26</sup>My heart is glad; my soul rejoices; my body is safe. Who could want for more? <sup>27</sup>You will not abandon me to experience the suffering of a miserable afterlife. Nor leave me to rot alone. <sup>28</sup>Instead, You direct me on a path that leads to a beautiful life. As I walk with You the pleasures are never-ending, and I know true joy and contentment.*

<sup>29</sup> My fellow Israelites, I can say without question that David our ancestor died and was buried, and his tomb is with us today. <sup>30</sup>*David wasn't speaking of himself;* he was speaking as a prophet. *He saw with prophetic insight* that God had made a solemn promise to him: God would put one of his descendants on His throne. <sup>31</sup>Here's what David was seeing in advance; here's what David was talking about—the Messiah, the Liberating King, would be resurrected. *Think of David's words about* Him not being abandoned to the place of the dead nor being left to decay in the grave. <sup>32</sup>*He was talking about* Jesus, the One God has raised, whom all of us have seen with our own eyes and announce to you today. <sup>33</sup>Since Jesus has been lifted to the right hand of God—*the highest place of authority and power*—and since Jesus has received the promise of the Holy Spirit from the Father, He has now poured out what you have seen and heard here today. <sup>34</sup>*Remember:* David couldn't have been speaking of himself rising to the heavens when he said, "The Lord God said to my Lord, the King,

[35]"Sit here at My right hand, in the place of honor and power, and I will gather Your enemies together, lead them in on hands and knees, and You will rest Your feet on their backs.'"*

[36]Everyone in Israel should now realize with certainty *what God has done*: God has made Jesus both Lord and Liberating King—this same Jesus whom you crucified.

[37]When the people heard this, their hearts were pierced and they said to Peter and his fellow apostles,

**Pilgrims** | Our brothers, what should we do?

**Peter** | [38]Reconsider your lives; change your direction. Participate in the ceremonial washing* in the name of Jesus the Liberating King. Then your sins will be forgiven, and the gift of the Holy Spirit will be yours. [39]For the promise *of the Spirit* is for you, for your children, for all people—even those considered outsiders and outcasts—the Lord our God invites everyone to come to Him. Let God liberate you from this decaying culture!

Peter was pleading and offering many logical reasons to believe. [41]Whoever made a place for his message in their hearts received the ceremonial washing*; in fact, that day alone, about 3,000 people joined the disciples.

---

2:35 Psalm 110:1
2:38 Literally, immersion, a rite of initiation and purification
2:41 Literally, immersion, a rite of initiation and purification

[42]The community continually committed themselves to learning what the apostles taught them, gathering for fellowship, breaking the bread, and praying. [43]Everyone felt a sense of awe because the apostles were doing many signs and wonders among them. [44]There was an intense sense of togetherness among all who believed; they shared all their material possessions in trust. [45]They sold any possessions and goods *that did not benefit the community* and used the money to help everyone in need. [46]They were unified as they worshiped at the temple day after day. In homes, they broke bread and shared meals with glad and generous hearts. [47]The new disciples praised God, and they enjoyed the goodwill of all the people of the city. Day after day the Lord added to their number everyone who was experiencing liberation.

*A*lthough this young and thriving church had no political influence, property, fame, or wealth, it was powerful. Its power was centered in living the gospel. The people valued one another more than any possessions. They came together as a large, passionate, healthy family where it was natural to pray and share all of life together. The kingdom of God was blossoming on earth as these lovers of God embraced the teachings of Christ. The church has since lost much of the beauty and appeal we see in Acts. It has become concerned with a desire for material possessions, cultural influence, and large congregations.

# CHAPTER 14

# Matthew

## HEROD AND JOHN; JESUS FEEDS 5,000

¹At this time, the ruler *of Galilee* was Herod *Antipas.* He began to hear reports about all that Jesus was doing.

²*Like the people of Nazareth,* Herod wondered where Jesus' power came from.

| | |
|---|---|
| **Herod** *(to his servants)* | He must be John the Teacher who washed ceremonially,* raised from the dead; thus His power. |

> *H*erod was quite concerned with the attention that John the Teacher was receiving, but he didn't want to spend precious political capital killing a reputed holy man. On top of that, Jesus was beginning to create an even greater problem for Herod.

³⁻⁵Herod's brother Philip had married a woman named Herodias, *who eventually married Herod.* John denounced Herod's marriage to her as adulterous. Herod was incensed *(not to mention a little fearful)* and wanted to kill John, but he knew the people considered John a prophet. Instead, he bound John and put him in jail.

⁶⁻⁷*There John sat until* Herod's birthday. On that night, *Salome,* Herodias's daughter *by Philip,* came and danced for her stepfather and all his birthday guests. Herod so enjoyed her dancing that he vowed to give her whatever she wanted.

---

**14:2** Literally, John who immersed, to show repentance

| **Salome**<br>*(after whispering<br>with her mother)* | [8]Bring me the head of John the Teacher and Prophet,* displayed on a platter. |

---

*T*his was not what Herod had expected—he'd imagined his step-daughter might ask for a necklace or maybe a slave.

---

[9]Herod still thought it unwise to kill John, but *because he had made such a show of his promise*—because he had actually sworn an oath and *because the scene was playing out* in front of *the watchful eyes* of so many guests—Herod felt bound *to give his stepdaughter what she wanted.* [10]And so he sent orders to the prison to have John beheaded, [11]and there was his head, displayed on a platter, given first to *Salome* and then passed on to her mother.

[12]John's disciples went to the prison, got John's body, and buried him. Then they went to tell Jesus.

[13]When Jesus learned what had happened, He got on a boat and went away to spend some time in a private place. The crowds, of course, followed Jesus, on foot from their cities. [14]*Though Jesus wanted solitude,* when He saw the crowds, He had compassion on them, and He healed the sick *and the lame.* [15]At evening-time, Jesus' disciples came to Him.

| **Disciples** | We're in a fairly remote place, and it is getting late; *the crowds will get hungry for supper.* Send them away so they have time to get back to the village and get something to eat. |
| **Jesus** | [16]They don't need to go back to the village in order to eat supper. Give them something to eat here. |

---

**14:8** Literally, John who immersed, to show repentance

| | |
|---|---|
| **Disciples** | [17]*But we don't have enough food.* We only have five rounds *of flatbread* and two fish. |
| **Jesus** | [18]Bring the bread and the fish to Me. |

*So the disciples brought Him the five rounds of flatbread, and the two fish,* [19]and Jesus told the people to sit down on the grass. He took the bread and the fish, He looked up to heaven, He gave thanks, and then He broke the bread. Jesus gave the bread to the disciples, and the disciples gave the bread to the people; [20]everyone ate and was satisfied. *When everyone had eaten,* the disciples picked up 12 baskets *of crusts and broken pieces of bread and crumbs. Not only was there enough, but there was an abundance.* [21]There were 5,000 men there, not to mention all the women and children.

[22]Immediately, Jesus made the disciples get into the boat and go on to the other side of the sea while He dismissed the crowd. [23]Then, after the crowd had gone, Jesus went up to a mountaintop alone (*as He had intended from the start*). As evening descended, He stood alone on the mountain, praying. [24]The boat was in the water, some distance from land, buffeted and pushed around by waves and wind.

[25]Deep in the night, *when He had concluded His prayers,* Jesus walked out on the water to His disciples *in their boat.* [26]The disciples saw a figure moving toward them and were terrified.

| | |
|---|---|
| **Disciple** | It's a ghost! |
| **Another Disciple** | A ghost? What will we do? |
| **Jesus** | [27] Be still. It is I. You have nothing to fear. |
| **Peter** | [28]Lord, if it is really You, then command me to meet You on the water. |

| Jesus | [29]*Indeed,* come. |

Peter stepped out of the boat onto the water and began walking toward Jesus. [30]But when he remembered how strong the wind was, his courage caught in his throat and he began to sink.

| Peter | Master, save me! |

[31]Immediately, Jesus reached for Peter and caught him.

| Jesus | O you of little faith. Why did you doubt *and dance back and forth between following* Me *and heeding fear?* |

[32]Then Jesus and Peter climbed in the boat together, and the wind became still. [33]And the disciples worshiped Him.

| Disciples | Truly You are the Son of God. |

[34]All together, Jesus and the disciples crossed *to the other side of the sea.* They landed at Gennesaret, *an area famous for its princely gardens.* [35]The people of Gennesaret recognized Jesus, and they spread word of His arrival all over the countryside. People brought the sick *and wounded* to Him [36]and begged Him for permission to touch the fringes of His robe. Everyone who touched Him was healed.

people. They laid them at His feet, and He healed ... people saw the mute speaking, the lame walking, *the ... whole*, the crippled dancing, and the blind seeing; and ... were amazed, and they praised the God of Israel.

32We must take pity on these people for they have touched My heart—they have been with Me for three days, and they don't have any food. I don't want to send them home this hungry—they might collapse on the way!

33We'll never find enough food for all these people, out here in the middle of nowhere!

34How much bread do you have?

Seven *rounds of flatbread* and a few small fish.

... the crowd to sit down. 36He took the bread and the fish, ... nks, and then He broke the bread and divided the fish. ... bread and fish to the disciples, the disciples distributed ... people, 37and everyone ate and was satisfied. When ... eaten, the disciples picked up seven baskets *of crusts* ... *pieces and crumbs. Not only was there enough, but there* ... *dance.* 38There were 4,000 men there, not to mention all ... and children.

...sus sent the crowd away. He got into His boat and went ...

# *Matthew*

# CHAPTER 15

## WHAT MAKES YOU CLEAN?

1Some Pharisees and scribes came from Jerusalem to ask Jesus a question.

**Scribes and Pharisees** | 2The law of Moses has always held that one must ritually wash his hands before eating. Why don't Your disciples observe this tradition?

3Jesus—*who was developing a reputation as One who gave as good as He got*—turned the Pharisees' question back on them.

**Jesus** | Why do you violate God's command because of your tradition? 4God said, "Honor your father and mother.* Anyone who curses his father or mother must be put to death."* 5-6But you say that one need no longer honor his parents so long as he says to them, "What you might have gained from me, I now give to the glory of God." Haven't you let your tradition trump the word of God? 7You hypocrites! Isaiah must have had you in mind when he prophesied,

8"People honor Me with their lips,
But their hearts are nowhere near Me.
9 Because they elevate mere human ritual to the
status of law,
Their worship of Me is a meaningless sham."*

15:4 Exodus 20:12; Deuteronomy 5:16
15:4 Leviticus 20:9
15:9 Isaiah 29:13

¹⁰(To the multitude) Hear and understand this: ¹¹What you put into your mouth cannot make you *clean or* unclean—it is what comes out of your mouth that can make you unclean.

¹²Later, the disciples came to Him.

| | |
|---|---|
| **Disciples** | Do You realize the Pharisees were shocked by what You said? |
| **Jesus** | ¹³Every plant planted by someone other than My heavenly Father will be plucked up by the roots. ¹⁴So let them be. They are blind guides. What happens when one blind person leads another? Both of them fall into a ditch. |
| **Peter** | ¹⁵Explain that riddle to us. |
| **Jesus** | ¹⁶Do you still not see? ¹⁷Don't you understand that whatever you take in through your mouth makes its way to your stomach and eventually out *of the bowels* of your body? ¹⁸But the things that come out of your mouth—*your curses, your fears, your denunciations*—these come from your heart, and it is the stirrings of your heart that can make you unclean. ¹⁹For your heart harbors evil thoughts—fantasies of murder, adultery, and whoring; fantasies of stealing, lying, and slandering. ²⁰These make you unclean—not eating with a hand you've not ritually purified with a splash of water *and a prayer.* |

²¹Jesus left that place and withdrew to Tyre and Sidon. ²²A Canaanite woman—*a non-Jew*—came to Him.

| | |
|---|---|
| **Canaanite Woman** *(wailing)* | Lord, Son of David, h... is possessed by a de... *mind is senseless! Ho...* |

²³Jesus said nothing. *And the woma...*ples came to Him.

| | |
|---|---|
| **Disciples** | Do something—she l... |
| **Jesus** | ²⁴I was sent here onl... Israel. |

²⁵The woman came up to Jesus and...

| | |
|---|---|
| **Canaanite Woman** | Lord, help me! |
| **Jesus** | ²⁶It is not right to wa... ing dogs. |
| **Canaanite Woman** | ²⁷But, Lord, even dog... the table as their mas... |

²⁸Jesus—whose ancestors included l... kindness and insight.

| | |
|---|---|
| **Jesus** | Woman, you have gre... done. |

And her daughter was healed, right th...

²⁹Jesus left and went to the Sea of G... taintop and sat down. ³⁰Crowds throng... lame, *the maimed,* the blind, the crippl...

*sick and bro...* them. ³¹The... *maimed ma...* the people ...

**Jes...** *(to His disciple...*

**Discipl...**

**Jes...**

**Discipl...**

³⁵He told ... He gave tha... He gave the... them to the... everyone h... and *broken...* *was an abu...* the women... ³⁹Then J... to Magada...